A Year with the Angels

Also available by the same author

Past Life Angels

Souls Don't Lie

Past Life (meditation CD)

The Tree That Talked

How to Be Happy

Forever Faithful

Supernaturally True

Pets Have Souls Too

Angel Whispers

Soul Angels

Everyday Angels

Angels Please Hear Me

Pets Are Forever

A Year with the Angels

JENNY SMEDLEY

HAY HOUSE

Australia • Canada • Hong Kong • India
South Africa • United Kingdom • United States

First published and distributed in the United Kingdom by:
Hay House UK Ltd, 292B Kensal Rd, London W10 5BE. Tel.: (44) 20 8962 1230;
Fax: (44) 20 8962 1239. www.hayhouse.co.uk

Published and distributed in the United States of America by:
Hay House, Inc., PO Box 5100, Carlsbad, CA 92018-5100. Tel.: (1) 760 431 7695 or
(800) 654 5126; Fax: (1) 760 431 6948 or (800) 650 5115. www.hayhouse.com

Published and distributed in Australia by:
Hay House Australia Ltd, 18/36 Ralph St, Alexandria NSW 2015. Tel.: (61) 2 9669 4299;
Fax: (61) 2 9669 4144. www.hayhouse.com.au

Published and distributed in the Republic of South Africa by:
Hay House SA (Pty), Ltd, PO Box 990, Witkoppen 2068. Tel./Fax: (27) 11 467 8904.
www.hayhouse.co.za

Published and distributed in India by:
Hay House Publishers India, Muskaan Complex, Plot No.3, B-2, Vasant Kunj, New Delhi
– 110 070. Tel.: (91) 11 4176 1620; Fax: (91) 11 4176 1630. www.hayhouse.co.in

Distributed in Canada by:
Raincoast, 9050 Shaughnessy St, Vancouver, BC V6P 6E5. Tel.: (1) 604 323 7100;
Fax: (1) 604 323 2600

© Jenny Smedley, 2011

The moral rights of the author have been asserted.

The author of this book does not dispense medical advice or prescribe the use of any
technique as a form of treatment for physical or medical problems without the advice of a
physician, either directly or indirectly. The intent of the author is only to offer information
of a general nature to help you in your quest for emotional and spiritual wellbeing. In the
event you use any of the information in this book for yourself, which is your constitutional
right, the author and the publisher assume no responsibility for your actions.

A catalogue record for this book is available from the British Library.

ISBN 978-1-84850-370-0

Printed and bound by CPI Group (UK) Ltd, Croydon, CR0 4YY

Dedication

I'd like to dedicate this book to all my readers, both past and future, in the hopes that my words might help them change their lives for the better.

My thanks to Hay House for their continuing trust.

My thanks, of course, to my best friend and husband, Tony, for giving me his total support and for being my perfect sounding board.

Angels don't know blame or judgement
— they know only love

— Jenny Smedley

Contents

Foreword

Angels are everywhere. To the believer there is little doubt that the angels whisper messages, influence circumstances, push people gently toward their goals, can save lives and even change the weather. Angels are loving powerful energy forces, the many-faceted aspects of the Divine Mind. Their very existence is in absolute service to the creation, and it is in adoration of God that they serve humanity, too.

Those of us who are working at some level with the angels, through writing, teaching, healing, etc., have also chosen at a soul level to be of service and, due to our very nature, have been chosen by the angels, too. Jenny Smedley is one such person, and through her devotion and hard work as a 'seed planter' she has strewn thousands of seeds all over the world, particularly in the form of ideas and encouraging words, giving readers the opportunity to come closer and closer to working with the angels, if they wish.

When your soul agrees to fulfil its purpose, there is a deep-rooted desire, a driving force within you (like an unsatisfied 'itch') that urges you to keep searching until you discover why you have chosen to be here.

That's exactly what happened to me. I had a very unusual childhood. Born to parents who were spiritually motivated to follow their individual life journeys – in separate directions – I was blessed with a life full of freedom and self-discovery. My adult life was different and held challenges caused by poor choices in both my marriage and career which took me away from my soul purpose which, in turn, led to depression and unhappiness. Then, having been re-introduced to living a life full of angels, I had a life-changing experience of huge proportions that led to a new understanding.

Angels are never far away. Even in the depths of our despair and heartache, the angels are there. They wait patiently for that moment when we eventually call out for help. Until that point they cannot intervene or influence our personal life choices uninvited. That would be a violation of our own free will.

Having changed my own life around in my early forties, I 'found the root of the itch' and I too became a healer and angel workshop facilitator, leaving nursing to follow a teaching programme that would encourage others to re-connect with their own spirituality. From that point of change I dedicated my life to help others find their angels, too!

How do we learn to connect with the angels? Through a deep desire to become part of the oneness that is creation itself. To let go of our own ego-centred way of being and allow the messages of the Divine Mind to work through us – often via God's messengers, the angels – in order to serve the greater purpose, for the best possible outcome of all and the highest good. Along the way, through subtle changes to our personality and through our own better decisions, the side-effect is that we also attract all that we need into our lives, lovingly.

Many of us are working together to raise consciousness and enable and empower seekers to make this angel connection. Whereas Jenny considers herself a 'seed planter', I think of myself as a match girl. I simply light the pilot light in someone's heart; I ignite the spark within. The flame of passion can then rise or fall in each individual allowing them to turn up the light, or not, at will. (It may be no coincidence that I found myself living in a Victorian factory conversion studio apartment in London which had once been the Bryant & May match factory!)

The angels can only work alongside us when we are ready to make the choice to raise our own vibration, and work at it. They can only work alongside us when we are prepared to smooth off some of our rough edges and become more consciously aware of the effect of our thoughts, words and actions. If our own vibration is too heavy, caused by too many negative attitudes, we are too 'dense' and prevent our light from shining clearly. It is our light, shining clear and bright, that the world needs so badly in times of turmoil and unrest. With the rapid approach of 2012, when, as some believe, humanity and our planet Earth will be given the opportunity to evolve into a higher state of consciousness and being, our light is needed more than ever before, so that the positive energy of love, joy and peace may flow, and life on Earth can become more heavenly, for all of us.

There are millions of people, worldwide, who are working in their own way to bring the light and love of the angels closer to our world. Our role as spiritual beings enjoying a human experience is to learn, share the beauty around us in all creation and fill our hearts with joy and love, because by doing so we can shine our glorious light and fulfil our true potential.

But we are all unique individuals and some of us may lose our way along the spiritual highway, finding angels only by seeking help through the many books available. Some find their connection by working with animals or children, or in serving others in the community. Others may live differently but find their connection with the angelic realms through their dreams, meditations and prayers. While not all of us lead what is commonly termed a 'religious' life, each one of us can broaden our mind to raise our level of awareness, become more conscious of the effect we have on others, learn to notice the interconnectedness between all things and put love into action.

Working with angels does become more involved the more you learn, and to those of us who have dedicated our life's work to helping others it can be great fun – sometimes physically and emotionally exhausting, but enormously rewarding.

When Jenny asked me to write this Foreword to her latest book, I was delighted. This is one of the pleasures of the work! To acknowledge and support one another actively in an area which can at times seem a rather strange way of life to the sceptic or non-believer is a super thing to be asked to do.

This is a great way to work with the angels, and here Jenny has introduced angels for each month and for individual days of the week, so that you can connect with the heavenly beings on a regular basis – not only by learning the names of the angels, but by trying some or all of the exercises and ideas she has suggested for you. You will be uplifted and I know you will be inspired, as I was, by some of the many moving stories from all over the world, from ordinary mums to a veteran of the war in Vietnam.

I often tell people how blessed I am that this is my life as well as my work. I thank God and the angels every single day for their presence and many blessings. Part of the delight and joy is constantly meeting the wonderful 'angel-lovers' from all over the world. People like Jenny and people like you. Thank you for being there to share all this with.

As you read and enjoy this, may you too find your perfect way to fill your life with the joy of the presence of the angels, and may they in return fill your life with blessings and love, in abundance.

With my love,

Chrissie Astell

Preface

Sometimes, as humans, we need a little help in connecting with our angels. That's because, despite how we'd like to be and think, we do live in a world that operates through apparently inescapable realism. This means that from an early age, in the UK anyway, we're encouraged to use our left (logical) brain. We're discouraged from following our dreams and told that the only way to progress is to work hard and earn a lot of money. We're told that we live in a world of constantly impending catastrophe, such as disease, war and natural disasters, and that the only way to control events is with logic and the rational realism of science. This sometimes makes it hard for us to find a way to our angels, because once logic is firmly established, it's hard to turn off. We can and do create our own reality, and so the doom-mongers among us can create the very disasters about which they worry so much. The flipside is that if we're 'light-workers' we can also create a reality, different and infinitely more pleasurable, by concentrating on the positive. To do this we need to use our right (imaginative/spiritual) brain.

By giving you the names for the angels (which they don't need) and by giving you a specific structure for each of the months of the year, my aim is to offer you something to grasp in a logical way that will in fact help you tread an esoteric path more easily. When we humans try to meditate – the most direct route to connecting with angels – we can find it hard to switch off the everyday thoughts of our logical, left brain. This 'switching off', though, is essential if we are to meditate successfully.

The structures provided in the chapters that follow actually give your left brain something useful to grasp. Then, while the left brain is concentrating on the particular name and function of the particular angel for that time, it won't be interfering with the right side of your brain. This will make it easier for you to switch off the conscious thoughts that might normally impede your right brain, and allow you to embrace your creativity and connection to the angels.

Introduction: My Year with Angels

I've often been told to trust the angels, and time after time I receive confirmation that this is truly the best thing to do. Trusting isn't always easy, though, and if you're going through a particularly tough time, it can be hard to accept that perhaps it's for the best. The difficulty is that we, as humans, are rarely able to see the 'big picture'. We find it impossible to put our own emotional responsiveness and fragility aside and see a universal view of our souls. But even this is how it's meant to be sometimes. People who have very hard lives are sometimes being given very trying circumstances to survive because they are highly evolved and need greater and greater challenges to overcome in order to continue progressing. These people can get comfort from their angels in order to endure, but it may be that they're still meant to experience the difficult stuff.

Other people can *change* what's happening to them, but they have to believe they can do so, with help from their angels. So always ask for help finding 'the best possible outcome'. That way you allow your angels to make whatever you need to experience – rather than what you might *like* to have happen – come about freely. If we can accept this, and trust that angels operate for our best 'big picture' outcome, then if the angels can, they will help make things easier. It's good to look back on the year, at its end, as when you do, you may well find that events which appeared negative at the time have evolved into blessings. If they haven't, you should try and take a 'helicopter view' of them, looking at them objectively and asking yourself, if someone else had this problem what would your interpretation be of the lesson they were meant to learn? Always bear in mind that in each lifetime we are here to learn above all else, and lessons are sometimes very uncomfortable – but the good news is that if you can accept them for what they are, the need for them will cease and your life can then change for the better.

Here's a brief account of some of my year with angels in 2010. It's a very good idea to keep an angel diary, making a note of all the things that happen to you and then looking back on it months later. That way you can often work out where you're meant to be going and what lessons you're supposed to be learning. And if you can do that, your life can move on at a much more productive pace. It's for that reason that I've actually produced an 'Angel Diary' – watch out for it in the shops soon.

JANUARY

My angels gave me a few minor but irritating health issues, which at the time were an annoying distraction, but as a result I changed my diet and now, looking back, I can see that they were necessary. To connect well with our souls, we have to keep a reasonably pure and healthy body.

FEBRUARY

My birthday fell in this month and I made a mental deal with my angels to become a year wiser rather than a year older. People do tend to focus on their age quite a lot, but if you look at your soul, rather than your body, you're probably at least several hundred years old, so earthly years are pretty irrelevant really. Looking back this has definitely helped me, because this year has been one of my busiest ever! To keep mental agility and a fresh mind, I've made sure that I've continued to find time to have a fairly strenuous walk up one of the Somerset hills almost every day.

MARCH

The most important event in March is easy to pinpoint, and has been for the past few years: my husband Tony has his check-up and I'm always focused on getting the right results. This year saw his third year all clear since his surgery, which is wonderful and I thank my angels for taking care of us.

In March we also decided finally to replace our old sofas, as by then they were 30 years old, having been re-covered about 20 years previously. I will say here that we followed our usual guidance when choosing some, so we were a bit dismayed when, 20 weeks later, they still hadn't arrived... but more about that later. As is often the way with angels, things often work out for the best, despite initial appearances to the contrary.

APRIL

In this month we rented a cottage in Norfolk to spend some time with our son and daughter-in-law. We've rented many, many holiday cottages in the past several years, and in most cases they've been a disappointment. Either they turn out to be on a busy road (and KC, our dog, is terrified of traffic), or the cottage is uncomfortable, with lumpy beds or upright chairs. Sometimes the 'garden' turns out to have been cleverly photographed and is actually the size of a postage stamp, or not secure so that KC can only go out on a lead. Sometimes the promised 'dog walks' are fine once you get to them but you have to cross a dual carriageway to get there, or they're nearby but you sink up to your knees in mud at every step! Occasionally there are very noisy neighbours in an adjoining pub that no one had thought to mention, with bright lights that keep you awake at night. These were the sort of things I wanted dearly to avoid this time. So I decided to let my angels choose the place, and then at least I could blame them if things went wrong!

The cottage they chose was located in a delightful three acres of garden. The gardens were full of bluebells (my favourite flower) and park-like, with wide grassed and treed areas. The only neighbours were the owners, who still lived in London all week, so we had the whole place to ourselves from Monday to Friday. There were several walks right on the doorstep which didn't even require KC to be on a lead, and there was a choice between the common, a woodland walk or a trek down to the beach across the common. The cottage itself was small but beautifully formed. It was the best holiday we'd had for a long time.

In this month I'd also been asked to do jury service, which was a bit inconvenient as I was asked to attend on the day after we drove back (six to seven hours) from Norfolk. I didn't exactly ask my angels to get me out of it, as that would have seemed a bit churlish of me, but they obviously got the message anyway, because on the day we were coming home I got a call on my mobile to say that not only did they have too many people, but some of them were very keen to be jurors, so would I mind dropping out?!

MAY

May is always the month that I love the best. This year I spent it just enjoying our one-acre garden, installing a pond for wildlife at the bottom complete with a weeping willow and planting a small wooded area with silver birch, horse chestnut, alder, pear and plum trees. We also had a large pergola built at the end of a hedge walk and covered it with Virginia creeper, clematis, hydrangea, honeysuckle and wisteria. We then put up a summerhouse for Tony to do his healing in. During all of this our angels were all around, because we were so content and happy.

I do many talks throughout the year, and in this month I did a rather special one in Exeter, at the One Vision Foundation, which deserves a special mention. When I do these talks, if I get it exactly right, angels come winging in and light up the people there, and that's what happened on this occasion. The questions the audience asked were insightful and intelligent and I had a wonderful time, so much so that I had to literally drag myself away at the end. I didn't want to leave!

JUNE

In June I shared an experience with my husband Tony, and his mum, which proved once again that angels can and will help when it's appropriate. We were in the car, driving Tony's mum back to her home in Essex after a week's holiday with us. This involved travelling at speed along fast roads for most of the way. It was a tedious journey that encouraged you to perhaps drive a little faster than you really wanted to. One thing kept us steady, and that was the fact that KC, our beloved dog, was strapped into her seatbelt on the back seat. At this particular part of the journey I'd changed places with Tony's mum so that she could sit in the front with her son. I was in the back with KC.

So, we were bowling along at about 65 miles per hour I would think, mostly lost in our own thoughts, dreaming away. Ahead I registered peripherally that there was a huge lorry parked at the side of the road. It was in a lay-by, but the edge of the parking area was right at the side of the road. This was the A303, on a section where it was a dual carriageway. As we got to within a few yards of the lorry, unbelievably it started to pull out into the road, right into our pathway. Either he hadn't seen us or he had seen us and assumed we'd pull onto the other lane and get out of his way. Ordinarily, I suppose this might have been fine, but for one thing: the lorry driver can't have seen that there was a car travelling alongside us, passing us. This pincer movement left us nowhere to go.

There was nothing anyone could do. There was no time to stop and things (especially the vehicles) were moving so fast toward inevitable impact that I was tempted to close my eyes. I didn't, though; I watched in horror as in a split second the vehicles all moved closer together. A thought flashed through my mind about KC. What on Earth would happen to her if she survived and we did not? I remember, as the back of our car came alongside the lorry, looking at the huge back wheels as they were dragged into the road by the front end, which was already inches from being in front of our car. The gap diminished as the lorry came out and the car the other side kept pace with us. It was already too late anyway because the gap we were heading for was too small for our car to get through, by a foot or so. I had no doubt that in a split second our car, with us inside, would be somersaulting down the road, a tangled mass of metal.

When I asked Tony about it later, he said that to him things had gone into slow motion, and we were sort of floating toward the gap into which he had no choice but to continue to steer, even though he knew it was hopeless. I felt enveloped by some sort of white light, and I recall at that moment going briefly into a state of complete acceptance. It's amazing how time seems to be able to stretch at moments like this, but of course angels are not constricted by time as we are. Then suddenly, it was all over. It was as if we and our car had become pure energy for a split second and we'd passed through a gap that was just too small for us to fit. Had we collided, I'm sure it could have been a fatal accident for all of us in the car, but instead we all sat there, in shock, ecstatic to have survived, but not understanding how, safely on our way. At that point, looking back through the side window I could see that the lorry driver had finally braked, halfway onto the road. I imagine he was reflecting on how he could possibly have just avoided killing some people.

In hindsight, I'm sure our angels performed a miracle and, because it was not our time, they transformed the car into fluid energy and squeezed it, like toothpaste out of the tube, through the gap between the lorry and the other car. It's not the first time we've been saved from a car crash, but it was truly the most amazing incident of them all to me.

So, in that 'final' moment, had I trusted? I do believe I had because while one part of my mind was certainly jumping ahead to the bang of impact, the tumbling down the road, hitting other cars and hearing the screeching tangle of tons of metal as it compacted around our fragile bodies, another part of me was tranquil and accepting, and so things were able to be changed by our angels.

JULY

In July we nearly decided to sell our house. Sometimes you love your home but the energy surrounding you isn't right. We had the same thing happen when we lived in a different part of the Somerset countryside. In that case it was the proximity of an abattoir a couple of miles away that put us off. But this bungalow was so special. We'd been helped and guided into buying it, against all the odds, and it didn't seem to make any sense that we should be driven out. In this case it was some neighbours who made us feel uncomfortable. I'm not going to go into details, but suffice it to say that we found the fact that their house was only about 20 feet from our main lounge wall, too close for comfort. We really didn't want to move, though – we'd put so much into the garden and would find it almost impossible to get another one like it. So, one night as I went to bed I asked my angels to find me a solution. Having the neighbours move would be one thing, but there'd always be new ones and you never know what you're going to get. We needed a permanent, foolproof solution. By morning I'd seen it all in my mind. Angels had shown me a lateral way. We would reconfigure the whole house. Our view, across the back garden, had always been one we didn't see except in summer from the conservatory, and this idea would change that, too. We were to chop up the existing lounge and make the front half into a new spare bedroom. This would put it – the least used room – closest to the house next door. In one corner we'd create an ensuite cloakroom. The back half would then be knocked through to the kitchen, making that into a kitchen/diner with a snug area in front of the old fireplace. Both kitchen and dining area sides of this room would front onto the conservatory. Then we'd create an office for me from the garage and create a whole new lounge, complete with wood-burner, from the old spare room, the utility room and my old windowless office on the other side of the house. This new lounge would have its long side facing the view, with patio doors.

It all sounded fabulous, but Tony and I have never been good at having builders in, and we'd never done such a big project so we really didn't know how it would go. Nevertheless, we drew up the plans and found a builder we were sure we could trust.

AUGUST

The building work went on through August. It was during this time that we realized why our sofas had been so delayed. If they'd come when they were supposed to, it would have been awful trying to move them (with their heavy cast-iron bases) all around the house to suit whatever work was going on. As it was, they wouldn't come until the work was finished and new carpets had been laid. What amazing foresight angels have!

Anyone who's had builders in knows what it's like: getting up early every morning for another day of dust, dust, more dust, noise and disruption. People had been very concerned when we told them what we were going to do, saying we'd never cope. It was traumatic and every single room was affected, and we often had nowhere to go. Even our bedroom was affected, because the builders had to go through there to get to the new office, which had once been the garage. The worst part was when the concrete floor in the garage had to be broken and removed to make it the same level as the rest of the house. The noise cannoned through the whole house, vibrating through. In the end, though, it wasn't me or Tony who had a nervous breakdown – it was my computer, which got so choked with dust that it ground to a halt!

SEPTEMBER

The building finished, we spent this month redecorating. I have a really hard time choosing colours and often make costly mistakes, so again I asked my angels to help. I wanted colours that would work on every dimension. They had to be colours that worked with the different light in each room, they had to be calming to the energy in each room and they had to look good, too! The added bonus is our new wonderful view from the lounge. I have a nice office with windows, and we have a lovely, large kitchen/diner. And all this just by rearranging the existing space, without having to extend. Brilliant!

OCTOBER

In October we decided we wanted cavity wall insulation on the one remaining wall that hadn't been done by the previous owner. I'll cut a long and fairly boring story short by saying that the company weren't willing to fit it without making a hole in the wall and inserting an air brick for ventilation. This would have made the room colder instead of warmer. We had visits from three different people from the company and each one said the same thing. So we gave up, but it was disappointing because the regulations to which they wanted to adhere made no sense at all. A couple of nights later I had a dream in which we were in a very snug house, so it was no surprise when we got a call from the company, with no explanation, saying that they were coming to put the insulation in without installing an air brick. We never did understand their change of heart, but I know some magical beings who perhaps have all the answers!

NOVEMBER

Angels sometimes have to make you take a step back before you can take a step forwards. This month we had the most frost and ice ever. The only thing to do was to enjoy the beauty of it, and it was the most incredibly beautiful natural display I've ever seen. More about this later.

DECEMBER

Things have gone so well this year work-wise that by this point I had to drop some of my regular commitments. I can't believe that in the last 15 years, just when I'd thought I'd achieved all I could, I've been given the chance to be in such a good position that I'm able to be selective about work. This Christmas will be spent giving thanks to my angels for all their help.

I had one new Christmas angel bonus this month when we put up some slate tiles behind our new wood-burner to protect the plaster. They were uncalibrated, which meant they were randomly coloured, very dirty and roughly cut. It wasn't until they were up, grouted and cleaned that I saw that on the top tile there was a perfect angel, in red, complete with halo and wings. You can see a picture of it on my Facebook page.

MORE ABOUT ME AND MY ANGELS

For one chapter of this book I decided to interview some of our recognized angel experts, asking them all the same questions, because I felt instinctively it would be very interesting to see if they gave corroborating answers. In some of their answers there are some excellent snippets of new revelations as well as confirmation of some other issues. It also serves to demonstrate that there are many different paths to the same truth. It was while I was doing this that a reader on my Facebook page said that I, too, should put myself 'on the spot' and answer the same questions. I agreed with her, and you can see the results on page lx.

MY JOURNEYS WITH ANGELS

The more I've thought about it, the more I realize that my angels really do come to me a lot during journeys. Readers of my other books already know that I had one visitation on a plane, one on a train and several near misses in cars that have undoubtedly been angel interventions. I recall yet another two incidents that occurred when Tony and I hadn't long been married. They both happened on the same road, in the same spot and in the same car!

At the time we had a gold metallic Triumph Herald. Nowadays a classic, we loved the chunky build and sleek profile of this car, which at the time was a bit of a 'banger'. The first time, we were driving down a road called Springhouse – bizarrely, a road my parents moved to many years later. When things become connected like this, you really have no choice but to understand that this is angelic synchronicity at work. Anyway, one night we were driving down this road over a thick sheet of snow and ice in our Triumph Herald. We probably shouldn't have gone out at all, but youth can be very foolish! We were approaching the main road junction. The road ahead had been gritted and wasn't anywhere near so dangerous, but it still had a thick coat of slush on it, making it slippery. Tony braked gently as we approached the junction, but the car just sailed serenely onwards. Realizing we weren't going to stop in time, Tony tried to steer us toward the edge of the road, hoping the kerbstones would stop us, but the steering had no effect on our direction whatsoever. The road we were on was quite a steep one, so we picked up speed as we slid toward the junction. Ahead, traffic flowed along the main road with barely a break. Neither of us said anything as our eyes gaped at the traffic going by and searched in vain for a gap that might allow us to slide to safety. We reached the edge of the snow and the car ploughed on ahead into the slush, the steering and brakes coming back online a little too late to help us.

Magically, the traffic parted before us as a gap appeared, seemingly from nowhere. With quick thinking, Tony allowed the car to continue straight across the road and into the turning opposite, thus taking us out of the path of danger.

A bit of luck, you might think, but a few months later we had just pulled onto Springhouse from the main road when there was a loud bang and the back of the car dropped. If we'd still been on the main road we'd have been going a lot faster, and might have turned the car over, but as we were on a minor road, having just slowed right down for the turning, there was no problem. We got out and stared in disbelief at the half-axle, wheel still attached, which now lay next to the car. That was the end of our much-loved car, but at least it wasn't the end of *us*!

Writing this reminds me of yet another incident that happened a few years after that one. This time we were in a Ford Cortina, driving along the A13, which is now a dual carriageway but back then was fast, with a pretty bad reputation for being dangerous. As we rounded a gentle bend, Tony driving (back then I hadn't learned to drive), we were both totally horrified to see an oil tanker charging straight at us on our side of the road. I don't know what on Earth the driver had been thinking, but he'd obviously made a rash decision to overtake a queue of slow-moving cars. There was no doubt we were going to crash head-on, and with a vehicle that size we'd have had no chance. But at the last second we suddenly swerved aside into a bus stop which Tony, somehow, had had the presence of mind to notice. We described a short, fast arc into the bus stop, neatly allowing the tanker to pass before we slipped back onto the road and sailed on as if nothing had happened. The odds of that short gap being right there at the right split second must be phenomenal. No wonder I see angels in Tony, as they so often seem to operate through him!

These incidences are just some of those I've experienced while travelling. Others have been recounted in other books. Of course I've pondered over this 'travel' connection, or rather 'journey' connection, which is what I've decided it is. I have a lot of trouble being patient. I know that we're meant to enjoy each and every moment of each and every journey on which we're taken, but literally and figuratively I have a big problem with always wanting to reach my destination. We all know that looking back from journey's end is often not as interesting as looking forward, so I hope I'll conquer this fault in time. This reminds me to say something about dreams and hopes, because they too are very much a journey of a kind. We travel from the inception of a dream to its achievement. In the case of an aspiration it's very important indeed to enjoy the journey. Dreams, once attained, are no longer dreams, and every dream has its issues and sometimes problems. The journey toward success is often the best part of attaining a dream. When something we dreamed of doing becomes a reality, in time it loses its dream quality and becomes something we can take for granted – so enjoy all your journeys, pause often and look back at how far you've come!

I've mentioned before how nowadays Tony follows his own procedure for keeping us connected to our angels while we're in the car, and how that seems to help protect us. What he does (and anyone can do this), is visualize a bubble of white light around the car. He's been doing this for so long now that for him it's become second nature, and so very easy. It will take anyone starting this a while to get to that point, but my advice would be to keep trying. The good thing is that once you get this virtual bubble in place, it's very easy to check that it's working. As you drive down the road you'll notice, when your protection is in place, that other cars don't crowd yours as much as usual. They don't tailgate you and other drivers are more inclined to let you out of turnings, etc. Speed-merchant type idiots are less likely to overtake you in dangerous places, and your own driving seems to improve as your hands seem to become 'guided' on the wheel. I often wonder what the result would be if everyone in the country tried this out on the same day. Think about it. Road safety, I am sure, would be vastly improved on that day, either by others driving more carefully around you, or by you being imbued with the 'luck' and lightning reflexes that have saved me and Tony many times. I honestly believe that the road safety records would prove once and for all that angels do exist and will help us under the right circumstances. It would be a fascinating experiment, wouldn't it?

Famous Angel Experts

We've all got our favourite angel expert, and lots of people have told me that they'd like to sit down with their favourite over a cup of coffee and discuss all things angelic with them. I wanted to talk to some angel experts and ask them some questions which I thought my readers would like to ask if they had the chance. I interviewed several and it was very interesting how many answers were similar, but also even more interesting to read the diverging ones. I hope you'll enjoy reading the words of these recognized experts and that they'll give you some insight into your own possible angelic connections.

Jacky Newcomb
– *The Angel Lady* and Fate & Fortune's *Angel Expert*

> I think I wanted angels to be real my whole life. As an adult I started to investigate the phenomenon with gusto and I think it was the sheer volume of real-life stories which really tipped the balance. So many people wrote to me from all over the world with their angel encounter

experiences, and many of them were just impossible to write off. I knew angels must be real from that time and I invested my time sharing what I had learned and teaching others about angels.

One day I was watching the UK daytime magazine show *This Morning* and the guest was a woman called Diana Cooper. She had just written a book about her own angel encounter, and as I listened to her I realized that I'd had my own angel experience as a child. Aged about five years old I'd got into difficulties in the sea; separated from my parents, I was only meant to be rinsing the sand off my hands but went into the water. I found myself being dragged out to sea by the rough waves, and at the moment I considered that I might actually drown, I knew I was no longer alone. An angelic voice offered to take care of me and I felt I was assisted back to the water's edge. The whole memory came back to me at that time as if the programme had been a trigger.

Once the show finished I went out and bought Diana's book, but then had a thirst for more. Over the next 12 months or so I read everything I could find about angels. We also had early Internet access at a time when we knew no one who even had home computers, so I was able to search online. Surprisingly, even in the very earliest days of the Internet there were people posting about angels. I created my own website and before I knew it, people were writing to ask me about angels and I was able to help.

Later I wrote my own book, and then more. The more you learn, the more you want to teach and the more there is to teach. I've had 11 books published so far, with several more in the pipeline, on themes of angels, the afterlife and positive paranormal experiences. There is so much more to the world around us than we can possibly imagine!

I had a lot of help in my quest to follow my path. I decided I wanted to write my own book about other people's angelic encounters, and the publisher literally came to me. It took a lot longer to write the book than I thought and so I started to write a few articles and later became a columnist for a brand new magazine, *Chat – It's Fate* (I'm now with *Fate & Fortune* magazine).

I did have a promotions and marketing background, and I still had to work at my success, but I felt as though angels were helping me every step of the way. Everything felt comfortable, as if I were literally following the path I had agreed to before birth. This is my life's mission – I know it deep in my heart.

Angels will appear in dreams; although to be fair they don't normally look like you would expect angels to look (no wings!). But sometimes I just wake up and whole concepts and ideas for my work are just sitting in my mind waiting for me to go and write them down. I've even woken up with book titles and simple instructions. One funny one was 'eat pomegranates' (I don't like them, actually, but I assume the juice must be good for my body so I drink it whenever I can).

Other times I get a strong 'knowing' about something, and the angels even give me premonitions both for myself and others – usually family members. They don't normally give me advice for strangers – I believe my role is that of a scribe or record-keeper and teacher rather than a psychic and reader.

I think it helps if you believe in angels, but you don't have to! But why not take a chance? Talk to your own guardian angel and ask for signs that they are around you. They like to bring people white feathers as gifts and some-times small coins. Angels don't have free will in the same way that humans do. They can't interfere in our lives but can help... if we ask them for help. You don't need lots of fancy rituals (unless you enjoy this sort of thing, and I've written books with lots of ideas if you want to do this).

Wear an angel pin or use angel-decorated products in your home. Surround yourself with their images. You don't have to spend loads of money, and in fact I sug-gest you don't, but you could make things yourself or ask for them as gifts. I have angels on everything – I really immerse myself in my work!

Meditating is helpful. Try asking your angels a question before you go to sleep at night – you might be amazed at the answer you get. I like to keep an angel journal, too, (several actually) and write down positive things that happen in my day. You can record your angel experiences, write poems, stick in pictures of angels or just write down compliments you've been paid or magical experiences that people share with you... anything which lifts you. I firmly believe that if you appreciate the good things in life, more of them will flow your way.

We're all going through a change based on the planet raising its rate of vibration. It's happening right now. Angels are gathering closer at this time and we're all part of the plan. We need to be living in a state of love and tolerance, helping others. Many will have noticed occasional psychic experiences in their lives and the lives of people around them. These experiences will become more commonplace. If you are already reading books like this then you are already on the path. Recycling, taking care of the planet – these are things that are important right now. The angels are helping us. Watch for things which excite you (these are the things you should be doing). We all have our own individual skills, so don't feel you have to 'save the whales' if you spend each weekend helping at the children's centre. Don't worry too much about what you are *meant* to be doing... you're probably already doing it.

Some people believe that angels are closer during times of grief and loss, pain and illness or when we are in danger. I think angels are close when we need them, but they are always hovering, just out of sight, waiting to be called by us. If you want to work with angels then they are always going to be around... particularly during these important Earth changes. Just ask for their help and know that they are supporting you.

Alexandra Wenman
– Editor of Prediction *and Angel Expert for this magazine*

I have always believed in angels. My mum – who is a Catholic, but also very spiritual and psychic – used to help me pray to them for protection and guidance when I was very little. I have just always felt protected and watched over, and when I was young I knew that if I prayed hard enough I could manifest the things that I needed. In my teenage years I became really interested in all manner of spiritual subjects – I dabbled in Wicca and Tarot and developed a huge love of working with crystals, which I still use today in my crystal layout work.

When I first moved to the UK, when I was just 21, I went through a terribly difficult time. I was in an unhappy relationship, far from home, my career as a journalist stalled and, as an Aussie, I really struggled with the cold weather and darker days and nights. I battled depression off and on for a good few years and totally turned my back on my spiritual side – mainly to please my controlling boyfriend, but also because I just couldn't seem to see any light at the end of the tunnel. I now know that if you choose to see it, it's certainly there. My re-awakening came on my first visit home to Australia, after living here for two years, when my mum gave me Diana Cooper's book *Angel Inspiration*. As soon as I started reading the book, I began to see incredible signs that the angels were with me. White feathers would appear as if from nowhere and I would see the word 'angel' written on signs, T-shirts – everywhere I looked. It was as if they were shouting out: 'We're still here! We haven't forgotten you.'

That's when I started asking them for help again and, miraculously, life changed for the better. I left my boyfriend, my magazine career got back on track and I really started to fall in love with living in England. I managed to get some freelance work with *Spirit & Destiny* magazine and decided that I'd love to do more of that type of thing. Although I took a full-time job at *NOW*, a celebrity magazine, I still did some freelance writing for a few of the spiritual magazines.

In the meantime I decided to work on my inner self to combat my depression and also to get to the bottom of why my romantic relationships never seemed to work out. After trying counselling and hypnotherapy, about two years ago I stumbled across a healing technique called Theta Healing. One of the exercises on the Theta Healing course was learning to do angel readings. Let's just say, I took to it like a duck to water! I was doing a reading for another woman in the class and asked to see which angel was with her and helping her at that moment. Suddenly, an immense golden angel materialized right behind her. He was sparkling and glowing in bright gold light and he was so big I couldn't get a handle on his actual size – but he seemed out of this world. I asked him his name and heard a booming voice say, 'Metatron.' I had heard of this angel before, but didn't know much about him. He reminded me of a giant Transformer, like in the film, as he seemed very angular. But then I realized he seemed to be made of sacred geometric shapes and he showed me a cube, which he passed through this woman's chakras one by one to balance and cleanse them. When I told her what I was seeing, she confirmed that she too felt that Metatron was with her. This was my very first experience of channelling these magnificent beings.

Another fellow Theta healer, Sabi Hilmi – who was assisting on the course – had been standing on the opposite side of the room and when I began my angel reading she leapt up from what she was doing and ran over to me. She told me later that she saw the whole thing and had to tell me how much the angels wanted to work with me. She told me I especially needed to develop my writing. We are now great friends!

I had a lot of angelic help on my quest to follow my path! The angels are with me every step of the way – every single day. I am now the editor of *Prediction* magazine (the UK's longest-running Mind/Body/Spirit publication – since 1936). I write my own angel column for *Prediction* and I have just set up my own Angel Healing, Theta Healing and Angelic Reiki business at www.angelic-intervention.co.uk. I will never turn my back on the angels or my spiritual path again. The angels have even helped me manifest my soulmate. My angelic experiences are really varied. Usually, I see feathers or signs in the physical world that they are with me, but I also receive messages in my dreams and I can also just sense or feel when certain angels – especially the archangels – are around me. On a few very special occasions I have channelled the most incredible beings, without even trying to. Once, archangel Michael appeared to me in St Mary's Cathedral in Sydney, and the mighty Melchizedek – the granddaddy of the archangels – popped up while I was travelling on a bus to work! I didn't know who he was, but I asked his name and then Googled it when I got to work. I was blown away that such a powerful being chose to visit me. I discovered Angelic Reiki after archangel Raphael visited me and showed me how he could integrate himself with my body to channel healing through my hands. I did some research and discovered that Angelic Reiki was exactly what he was showing me.

In all these channelled experiences, one thing remains the same: I am filled with the most unbelievable feeling of unconditional love and the visions are always accompanied by the most beautiful light. It is almost overwhelming and it sends tingles or a sparkling sensation throughout my entire being. I know instantly who is with me and I can feel their personality as though it were my own. I have written about these experiences in my column 'Archangel Alchemy' for *Prediction* magazine and I cannot wait to have more of them and connect in this way to even more angels!

My advice to other people on how to get closer to their angels is, just ask. The best advice that the angels have given me is that you have to ask for their help, otherwise they are powerless to intervene in a situation. Unlike

Famous Angel Experts

us, they do not have free will so you must remember to ask and then let go of any expectations or worries about the outcome. Surrender and release your worries to the angels and these will be resolved in miraculous ways.

There is a lot of talk about 2012 being a period of ascension for humanity and I really believe that more and more angelic humans – or 'Earth angels' – are being born right now to help us with this process and to usher in more peace to our world. For believers in angels, things like the credit crunch are a necessary adjustment period so we can get used to not relying so much on the material things in life and learn to help our fellow human beings on this planet. If you choose to focus on the positive, you will see all of the good coming out of these situations. Earth angels are being called upon to help others grow spiritually in order to 'ascend' more easily. We are entering a new era of peace, and I also believe that people are now learning that they no longer need priests and gurus – everyone is psychic and everyone is a healer. It's just whether or not you choose to tap into that birthright and use it for the greater good. The angels are a constant in my life – there's certainly never a time I feel there are fewer of them around. But I do feel that around the time of my birthday, in late September, I seem to experience even more of their love and

xlvii

blessings. Everything seems to line up for me at this time and I feel extremely blessed to be on this planet. New experiences pop up and issues get resolved. I've always loved my birthday as it feels like a great time of celebration, of peace, and of loving life and everything on this planet. I give thanks for all the wonderful people and experiences in my life. It reminds me that I have a purpose here, and I feel like the angels are letting me know that on my birthday. It's like they are giving thanks for me as well and it makes me feel extremely proud to be in their service.

Diana Cooper
— Teacher and author of many bestselling books

When I was a child, my parents ridiculed anything religious, spiritual or psychic, so I learned to close down and came to believe only in what could be seen, heard, touched or proved. It seems strange that with this background, when I was in my forties and in despair about my life, I threw myself into a chair with the words, 'If there's anything out there, show me.' A six-foot tall golden being appeared and took me on a journey to show me my future. That was when I knew angels were real.

I spent the next ten years on a spiritual seek-and-search. The angel had shown me a vision of myself on a platform talking to hundreds of people and told me I was to be a spiritual teacher.

Suddenly, there was a huge and fascinating spiritual world to explore and at the same time I knew I had to look within myself for self-understanding and also purification.

In my quest I trained to be a hypnotherapist, healer and counsellor. I read everything I could lay my hands on and listened to as many spiritual people as I could. I visited ashrams and, most of all, I meditated.

Ten years after their first visit to me, the angels returned and asked me to work with them and to tell people about them. It was only when I agreed to this that my life changed again. The very next week, after I said I would tell people about the angels, 50 people turned up to my evening class. Every one of them felt or saw their guardian angel that night. My mission had started.

The angels asked me to write a book about them. Suddenly they appeared during almost every hypnotherapy session to give me information and healing to include in the book. So it was that I wrote *A Little Light on Angels* (which has since been updated to *New Light on Angels*) and sent it to the publishers of my earlier books. They didn't want it, so I put the script in a drawer. A few weeks later, the angels asked me to send it to Findhorn Press to arrive the following Tuesday. I did so and Findhorn phoned the next day to say they wanted to publish it the following year. Something prompted me to say it would be good if it was out for Christmas. I was politely told that that was impossible, so I replied, 'Well, if the angels want it out for Christmas, they will see that it is.' Five weeks later, in good time for Christmas, the published book was in my hands.

The help given by the angels takes many forms. They wanted to catch the attention of people who were ready to wake up to angels. I was invited to appear on Richard and Judy's morning TV programme, and before we went on air the producers asked me if I would have my aura photograph taken. Naturally, I agreed and automatically asked my angel to step into my aura, thinking the viewers would sense the angel's energy. My angel impressed itself onto my aura photograph and hundreds of thousands of people saw it and phoned in to talk about angels! That was how those great beings of light helped me to be recognized as an angel 'expert', though they are such ineffable beings I don't know how anyone can be an expert on them!

Soon after that, they guided me to run an annual worldwide angel day, and on the first World Angel Day 1,000 people gathered in London and attended angel events all over the world. The energy was extraordinary! Now the annual angel day has been taken over by the Diana Cooper School and is called Angel Awareness Day.

The angels have assisted me in all sorts of ways. One of their strongest teachings is, 'Ask us for help.' You can ask for anything, small or large, and as long as it is for the highest good, they will give it. One time a friend of mine was dying. The doctors said there was no hope. I sat with lighted candles holding her in the light and calling on archangel Raphael, angel of healing, to help her. Suddenly I felt this huge surge of emerald light go through me as archangel Raphael himself came through me and went to her. She made a total recovery.

On another occasion, I decided to move house to live nearer the ocean. I chose a location and a friend of a friend offered to put me up and take me house-hunting. I told the angels what I wanted. We only looked at one house and it was perfect, but we realized it was much too big and much too expensive. Over dinner I completely let it go and we discussed looking for something smaller. That night I was woken at 4 a.m. by an angelic voice saying, 'Diana. That's your house.' I went down to breakfast and my friend rushed in, full of excitement. 'Diana, I was woken at 4 o'clock this morning by an angel saying, "Tell Diana that's her house."' So I bought it, despite a few challenges. When I moved in, I had a huge mortgage and £2,000 in the bank. The next day, bills totalling £10,000 arrived. I stood in the kitchen and said aloud, 'Angels, if you want me to live here bring me the money to pay these bills. If not, I'll put it on the market again and sell it.' The full amount came to me within two days! The angels are amazing.

What I did not know was that they had led me to an area of the UK that is full of angel energy, including elementals and unicorns, and that I was to meet them all on my journey.

As the years passed, I was delighted and privileged to meet many beings of the angelic realms. One day a unicorn came to me as I sat in the garden. He told me that his kind were returning to Earth now for the first time since Atlantis to help humanity. Known as the purest of the pure, these wonderful seventh-dimensional ascended horses help bring the visions of the soul to fruition. I often see them and always call on them to assist me and everyone.

One of the most exciting tasks the angels have given me is to tell people about orbs, which are the sixth-dimensional light bodies of beings of the angelic realms, caught on film. I was with my friend Kathy Crosswell when the angels arrived to tell us they wanted us to write about orbs. When we protested that we knew nothing about them, they said they would train us. After that we were given daily lessons on how to recognize them and interpret their messages. Orbs are constantly changing as the angels find new ways to work with our technology to give us visible proof of their presence.

One day we were writing about orbs when the energy became still and the candles went dim, as if some very high-frequency being was trying to reach us. It was a Seraph – one of those who surround the Godhead and sing into creation the thoughts of Source. It was a most awesome experience.

Every time you think about an angel, you are connecting with its frequency. So the more you think, talk or meditate about angels, the closer you become to them and the easier it is to tune in. Most people feel that they should see or feel something tangible. However, the connection is nearly always energetic and you have to trust it. Simply know that when you call on your angel or archangel, they are with you.

We are moving into stormy and exciting times as our planet ascends to a higher frequency. Light that is too high a frequency for our range of vision is pouring into us, shaking us up. It is also detoxifying Earth as we prepare for the new Golden Age starting in 2032; this will manifest as challenges. If you believe in angels and ask for the help needed by yourself and others, they will assist your journey. Trust and faith are two of the mightiest energies to smooth your path.

It is easier to connect with angels where the energy is high. So choose to visit beauty spots, mountains, sacred sites, forests, rivers and oceans, and be still so that they can touch you. And at sacred times like Christmas, the portals of heaven open and high-frequency energy floods into the planet making it possible to sense and know of the presence of angels. If you walk through life holding the hand of your angel, your path will be safe, happy and guided.

Michelle Jones
— Angel Expert for It's Fate *magazine*

I grew up in a seriously haunted house; we had moved into it when I was three, and by the time I was five I was really scared of going to bed! I would have terrible nightmares in which I would be pursued by a horrible woman who would then melt in front of me... skin and flesh crisping and falling off...

I found out many years later that the previous occupant of our home had committed suicide by setting fire to herself in the back garden!

One night, after I had eventually fallen asleep, I had the most incredible, wonderful dream... I was visited by an incredibly tall angel who took me from my bed and transported me to a huge hall, with golden pillars and an arched ceiling painted with stars. He put me down and held my hand as we walked toward another two angels standing nearby; I cannot remember what was said, only that I was being 'handed over' to the other two angels. I knew that these were my guardian angels and that they would help to keep me safe from the malignant presence in my house; they also promised that I would find a talisman to keep with me. When I awoke the following morning, there was a yellow plastic kazoo on my pillow! Now, I know that sounds like a very cheesy talisman, but I was only five – and that kazoo stayed with me for years!

Like many others, my life has had its high and low points. By 1995 I had built a successful career in personnel and training management, but I was incredibly stressed; I was chasing between work, childminders and school runs, as well as running our family home! I had absolutely NO time for me whatsoever... sound familiar?

In May 1995 I was involved in an accident that left me on crutches for 18 months, stuck at home. I was unable to move around much and rapidly becoming bored, despite having two young children and a third on the way! But I believe there is a reason for everything, and the break from chasing my tail gave me the space once more to hear messages from spirit and from my guardian angels. I had never actually spoken about any of this to anyone, not even my husband, and there were times when I wondered if actually I wasn't just plain nuts! Then, later in 1995, we went online for the first time and I discovered that if I was nuts, so were millions of other people! This gave me the courage to come a-creeping out of the broom cupboard and I spent some time learning more about communicating with spirit and training to become a healer. I thought my path was in the healing arts, but the angels thought otherwise and sent me another lesson to get me back on track!

In 2004 I was diagnosed with breast cancer and had to have chemotherapy, a mastectomy and reconstruction (I had seven operations in all). Oddly, I never felt the least fear that I would not survive. The treatment was tough but bearable and my surgeon is a miracle worker! The experience was very life affirming; it brought my family even closer together and taught me to enjoy the NOW and not worry about the future so much.

And of course, during the long months of recovery just about the only work I could do was write or work online. I was an active member of several online spiritual communities, helping others on their path, and then (on Jacky Newcomb's advice!) I began to send articles to MBS magazines. A stroke of fate led me to meet someone who knew that the newly published *Vision* magazine was looking for writers and I was lucky enough to be taken on as a regular writer and columnist. I have done quite a bit of radio, a teeny bit of telly (on Nuts TV!) and written loads of articles for magazines as well as publishing my own e-books via my website, and I firmly believe the angels have helped me with this because they want their message to be out there.

Every time I have become carried away with something which might distract me from what I am supposed to be doing, the angels have guided me back to the right track.

Sometimes I might have a particularly powerful dream; I dreamed of visiting holy wells in Cornwall about six months before I found the book that inspired me to go looking for them (*Secret Shrines* by Paul Broadhurst), or I may find that things just happen to fall in my way, for example when I met Jacky Newcomb in Penzance in October 2005 – a meeting that has led to us becoming firm friends. The accident in 1995 was a major blessing; without that I would never have put one foot on this path!

I will say, though, that if you ask the angels for the opportunities to come to you, you have to be ready to take them, and that can require courage.

You can get closer to your own angels by talking to them and listening for the answers! We cannot communicate with anyone on this Earth unless we make the effort to talk to them; why should this be any different for angels? When I was a child in the 1960s, the idea of talking to friends via a mobile phone was straight from science fiction, but now I can post a photo on Facebook and have friends who live in New Zealand comment on it in seconds! If we can believe in that, why not believe that there's an incredible dimension full of angels, who watch over us and help us through our lives?

The key to becoming close to them is so very simple: believe in them. Talk to them. Listen and watch for their reply; they never let us down.

I believe that we are gradually becoming more spiritually aware as a part of our evolutionary path and that the angels are helping us achieve this. If we embrace this and open our hearts and minds to them, who knows what humankind could achieve in the future?

I don't believe that there is a specific time when angels are closer, but I do believe that each person may feel an affinity to a certain part of the year, so that they are able to connect more easily.

I absolutely love the period leading up to Christmas, for all sorts of reasons; I love the crisp cold, the autumn colours, the sparkly frosty mornings and glittery cold nights – I even love the wind, rain and fog! Of course, my birthday is on Christmas Eve, so maybe that has something to do with it!

For me, I feel that the invisible world is just a heartbeat away for most of the year... but from October to the end of December, it feels even closer. You have to work at it, though; I make sure I spend some time outside as often as I can, as it helps me to stay grounded and recharge my 'spiritual batteries'. I am constantly talking to anything out there that is not bored with me constantly wittering on (!) and – this is the important bit – I listen, and watch, for the responses.

Let me leave you with this...

A short time ago I got in my car to drive into town and the radio wouldn't work. No amount of twiddling would help, so I started the engine and drove off. On my way, I was chatting away (out loud, but it's OK, as I was on my own in the car!) to my guardian angels about something that was on my mind and I asked for a sign that they had heard me. Then I apologized for asking for a sign again, for doubting that they were really there... but are you really there? You know how it goes!

I had literally just finished asking for the sign when the radio burst into life – just as Aretha Franklin sang the line 'I say a little prayer for you'!

I'll take that as a yes, then.

Jenny Smedley

I always thought about angels and tried to talk to them, right from a young age, when my priorities put me apart from many of my peers, but there was a pivotal moment when I got my proof of their existence. This was several years ago now, when I had my very first actual angel vision. Although I'd had messages before, I hadn't really understood where they'd come from. A vision on the train (which has been recounted in full in other books) was when I was shown my life's path – or rather I was 'offered' my life's path, as a choice out of three possibilities. I knew which one I was meant to choose, and of course I said yes, still not knowing to whom I was saying yes. In hindsight I should have realized who it was, because the amazing love I felt from this being was like nothing I'd ever experienced before. Anyway, it was afterwards when someone said to me, 'You realize you've made a contract with an angel?' that I finally understood that angels are very real indeed.

As soon as I accepted this 'contract', things started to happen to help me along my path. At first I didn't realize quite where it was leading, but amazing events such as being given my own TV show made me understand that I was being helped and guided, so I went where I was led. I've done this ever since. I was given the ability to create digital paintings of angels and to do remote aura readings, etc., in order that I would be able to write some regular columns for magazines. By doing this I was able to reach millions of people and try and 'plant a seed' in them.

I was also writing, but it wasn't until my publishers accepted my idea for my book *Angel Whispers* that I felt that angels and I had become officially linked. At that point I realized that I'd been guided to that 'recognition point' deliberately.

During another pivotal meditation I found myself standing in front of what I called 'The Council of 12'. I was looked into very deeply, on a soul level, and it was 'agreed' that I should continue.

I was constantly guided, herded by events, onto the right path. Acceptance isn't always easy, but it gets easier when you see the results of it. Angels always got me to the right place at the right time and introduced me to the right people also at the right time. Enquiries I've sent, which should in reality have been ignored, weren't, and step by step the angels brought me to where I am today. Angels have sent me little synchronistic signs for years, and I've always followed them. They led me to the home of my past-life husband, Garth Brooks, so that I could close the circle with him. They brought me into contact with Brian May, who has become a good friend. They led me to miss appointments and 'accidentally' bump into people. They've saved me from car accidents and helped a plane in which I was travelling when it got into trouble. I ask angels now to advise me every day.

Sometimes a specific song will come on the radio just as I've asked a question, and the words will give me my answer. Sometimes shapes will appear in the clouds or on car number plates. Sometimes there will be mishaps that make me late, and also make me miss a pile-up. Sometimes I'll get a message from my mum, through my angel, such as a shooting star appearing at a pivotal moment. Sometimes animals are sent, and their arrival gives me a positive sign.

Today, as I write, I'm waiting for the phone to ring to be a guest on an Australian radio show. I've no idea what questions will be asked or what answers I'll be expected to give. But I don't have to worry because my angels are right here, and they'll give me the answers I need at the right time. They always do.

To get answers and guidance from your own angels, be constantly aware of signs and messages in everyday occurrences. Try and keep a calm mind, which gives you a tranquil energy that makes it easier for the angels to come closer. Take photos if you feel that angels are near, as they will often show up as orbs or light effects. Take time to appreciate something beautiful, and always say thank you for it. Pass favours forward instead of keeping all for yourself. Anything that gives you a positive outlook, and therefore positive energy, will help. Ask. Always ask and always say thank you. Accept when you don't get what you want. All these emotional states will help you draw ever closer to the angelic realm.

For me it's always May when I most feel the presence of angels. I love the spring and the feeling of freshness and exciting possibilities that come with it. Pivotal things have tended to happen in my life during May, so I always welcome it with renewed expectations and a warm feeling that my angels are particularly close at that time.

I hope you've enjoyed these journeys through the worlds of a few of the people connected to angels as much as I have. I hope that maybe you see a way for you to emulate some of their methods and ideas. But these words should be taken only as a rough guide. Don't think for one minute that you have to do exactly the same as someone else or have the same experiences as someone else in order for them to be valid. Be open-minded, because, just as you are unique, your relationship with your angels is also unique.

January Angels

The New Year is time for a new start and new ways to connect with the angels, and what better way to start than with the angel of the month, Gabriel, the angel of communication?

Gabriel was said to be the angel in charge of the realm where Adam and Eve were first placed, and so this angel is very useful for making brand new starts. Gabriel is also the angel of the base chakra, so again ideal in creating firm foundations for the rest of the year. Start as you mean to go on!

NEW YEAR'S RESOLUTIONS

The beginning of the year brings us opportunities to change our lives. Angels are very keen to help us do this. Resolve at this time to stop worrying about things you can't change and make real steps toward changing what you can. This is a very good time to try some cosmic ordering, or an 'angel's shopping basket' as I like to call it. First things first, sit and think before you write out your list for the heavenly supermarket. There is a saying: 'Be careful what you wish for,' and it's very wise. Angels can

1

seem to think literally sometimes, so people can get what they ask for, but not quite in the way they meant. For instance, if you want to give up work, don't just write: 'I give up work.' You could get ill and have to retire, or you could have an accident, or find yourself having to care for an elderly relative, which won't be what you had in mind. Word things very carefully, so this wish should be something like, 'I receive a windfall of good luck which means I can live a more fulfilling life.'

Once you have it all straight in your mind, write your list down. Fold it up and place it inside a pouch or envelope with a cleansed crystal of your choice. (Cleanse the crystal by washing it in mineral water and leaving it to absorb the light of the sun and moon for 24 hours.) Meditate while holding the envelope or pouch and give your angels permission to start working on your wishes. If you do this regularly you'll find you can soon start crossing things off the list, as they come to reality.

You should also make a resolution to be more positive, and promise your angels that you'll try harder to create, continuously, the sort of atmosphere in which they're comfortable. Promise yourself that you'll think twice before moaning about someone or something in your life. If you can't live with them or it, do something to move away from that influence instead of just complaining about it.

The more you talk about something, or even think about it, the more importance and power you give it.

If last year was a disaster, try not to dwell on it too much. Draw a line under it and resolve to start again.

One of the ways to help your angels help you with this is to take your date of birth, for instance 4 February 1950, and add the numbers together, like this: $4 + 2 + 1 + 9 + 5 + 0 = 21$, then adding $2 + 1$ to get 3. Now add to that the digits that make up the new year. So if it were 2012, that would be $2 + 0 + 1 + 2$, which equals 5. Add the $3 + 5 = 8$. This means you are entering an '8' year. An 8 year is one of harvesting. It means that everything you've been trying to achieve for the previous seven years is coming to fruition. This is the time to succeed, or be ready for the following year which will be a time of letting go, surrendering and getting ready for a new start. This will be the year you discover if your dreams are going to become a reality. If this is the number you get when you add up your own date of birth and the year, then tell your angels that now is the time for them to really help you. Tell them that you are in an 8 year and they'll understand.

Here's a quick guide to what each number means for you:

1. a year for new beginnings
2. a year to build firm foundations

3. a year to learn and increase wisdom
4. a year to start teaching others and using your own wisdom
5. a year to stop and look backwards and reassess what you need to do
6. a year to be business-like and clear the clutter from your life and mind
7. a year for giant leaps forwards toward a real conclusion
8. a year to start manifesting success through attitude and reap rewards
9. a year to do or die, and grasp what you've achieved or let it go.

Many of my readers have listened to their angels and found their lives changing at this pivotal time of year.

Lynn's Story

I started my path to spiritual development last October when I quit my job of ten years in nursing, quite suddenly, knowing I should be doing something else. I was trying to develop my meditation skills, when one particular day in late January I just knew I had to go to Glastonbury. The urge was so strong that I got in the car and drove straight to Glastonbury, not knowing why I was going there. I started to look around the many interesting shops, when in one of them a shop girl asked me, 'Are you here for the psychic fair?' I said I wasn't, but she urged me to go along and I found a reader called Frances Munro, who blew me away. Frances told me that there were many angels around me, and they wanted to talk to me, and I must work with them. Since that day my connection to the angels has become stronger and stronger, and I do Angelic Reiki now. I know the angels have got more planned for me and I can't wait. It was definitely the angels that day, urging me to go to Glastonbury so I'd get the message.

I have contacted Lynn's angel who has imparted to me the name *Carmit*, which means 'small climber' in Hebrew. I think she's going to ensure that Lynn climbs slowly, patiently and persistently, just as she's been doing, like a grapevine that will one day reach the top.

Miriam's Story

I was a bad mother. I used to slap my kids and scream at them. I'd drink to take away my misery and take out on the kids the fact that their father had left us. One New Year's Eve I was sitting, the worse for drink as usual, crying, moaning that everyone was out celebrating and there was I on my own. I didn't remember much about my own parents. They'd handed me over to Social Services when I was about seven, I think. So, I'd lived a life in care, had no one that ever loved me and now I was trapped with three kids, so who was going to take me on? Talk about a pity party. I bathed in misery and gloom.

Then I fell asleep on the sofa and I had an awful dream. I dreamed that I was choking. I was gasping for air and trying to gag up something stuck in my throat. There were people all around me, but they took no notice. I was going to die. Just at that point in the dream when I thought I was a goner, I suddenly woke up as I was turned over and the stuff that was choking me (I'm sure you can guess that it was booze) spurted out of my mouth and I could breathe. Standing, cradling me, were my three little girls. Two of them were holding my arms, supporting me, while the other banged me on the back. I was mortified that they'd seen me like that, and that they loved me enough to help me when all I ever did was shout at them. They were all crying with relief that I was awake and breathing, and then they told me something that changed my life: they said that a beautiful lady had come to them. They'd been able to hear me gagging and were scared, but the lady told them not to be afraid, and to go downstairs. The kids said she told them what to do to help me. My skin pimpled into goose-bumps and I felt dizzy with a thrill

that maybe life really could be different. I'm not saying I
never shout anymore. I am human! But I try not to unless
I have to, and I've stopped drinking, except for a glass of
wine on special occasions. I started a new job and I have
faith that things are getting better. After all, I must have
been worth saving for something, mustn't I? And even
though the angel came to help my girls, really, rather than
me, it still means I'm worth something to them.

The angel that came to Miriam's children has given me the
name *Chryseis*, which means 'golden beauty' in Greek. I
think this angel will continue to watch over Miriam and
her family, and help her to fulfil her role as caretaker of
her children's souls, because that's what mothers really are.

Georgina's Story

Something happened to me in January last year that
turned my life around. The first was that I got attacked –
well, as near as makes no difference! I was coming out
of the mall late after having a look at the January sales,
and I was a little alarmed when I saw the parking lot was
almost empty apart from a truckload of guys all laughing,
and the worse for drink by the looks of them. They spot-
ted me and started making rude suggestions about me all
the while. I thought I had three choices: I could brave it

out and keep walking to my car, which was the other side of their truck. I could run to my car, showing my fear. Or I could run back inside the mall, again showing my fear but taking myself away from their direction. That's what I decided to do, but as I discovered, there's nothing as scary as an empty mall! The whole place echoed as I ran down between the stores, which all seemed to have their lights already off, or going off. It seemed like all the staff must have been leaving by back doors, because I didn't see anyone, least of all a security guard. When someone grabbed me from behind I started screaming. Next thing I knew I was surrounded and they were all grabbing a piece. I don't know how far they intended to go, but when I found myself being lifted bodily, I started yelling for God to help me. They started carrying me, over their heads, like some sort of weird trophy, back out to their truck. I knew that if they got me in there I'd be finished.

As they charged across the lot, whooping, I suddenly went cold. I wanted my mom. Mom and I hadn't spoken since she'd left my dad. I couldn't forgive her for ages, and then when I could, it seemed like it was too late, as she wouldn't answer my calls. I didn't know if she was mad at me or if she just figured I wanted to bad-mouth her and couldn't handle it. Either way, we hadn't spoken in months and months. But right at that moment, a little voice in my head told me she was the one I should call for, not God. 'Mom! Mom!' I started yelling, 'Help me!' No one took any notice because the parking lot was still empty save my car and their truck. We reached the truck and they started bundling me inside.

At that moment I saw a car pull into the lot and I couldn't believe it was the same model and colour as my mom's car. It parked right next to my car on the far side of the men's truck and it sat there, large as life. 'Mom!' I screamed. 'Mom! It's me!'

That made the men pause and there we were, with me halfway into the truck and what looked like my mom's car just sitting there. The car door opened and my mom stepped out. She held her cell phone in her hand and was saying loudly, 'So, officer, you'll be here in two minutes you say?'

Just like that the men dropped me and I hit the ground hard, winding myself. My mom ran over to me and fell down on her knees and she hugged me. It seemed like she'd missed me as much as I'd missed her, only we were both too dumb to have done anything about it. We sat there on the ground, rocking. She told me later she'd been driving home, along a highway about 500 yards from the mall. She had her windows up and the radio playing, but she said suddenly in her head she heard a voice. It said,

'Listen.' She turned the radio off and opened a window, and then she heard me calling for her. Somehow she knew where I was and next thing she was saving my butt. I'll never know who told her about me, but I'm told that Gabriel is the angel of communication, so maybe he set the whole thing up just to get me and Mom talking and making a new start together!

Georgina's angel has given me the name *Heti*, which comes from Sanskrit and means 'hot flame'. I'm sure that now her angel has brought them back together in this magical way, Georgina and her mother will burn forever as a guiding light to each other.

STRATEGIES FOR JANUARY
YOU DON'T NEED MONEY!

If your problems involve cash flow, don't ask for money directly, as angels don't use it and rarely understand our need for it! Just visualize the way your life would be and the things you'd do *if* you had more money, and then leave the 'how' up to your angels. Picture everything very clearly. For instance, if your dream is a new home, see it all: the front door, the garden, the furniture, curtains, everything, even down to the colour each room is painted. Make it real enough and your angel will make it so.

RESOLVE TO DO BETTER

Try to shut all negativity out of your life. Remember that we all can create our own reality. If we constantly think bad things and talk about bad things, then bad things are what will grow and materialize. If you find this difficult, then stop reading newspapers and stop watching the news. The media sensationalize bad news so that people will choose their TV channel or newspaper over others. It's business. If people tell you that by not watching or reading you're not being realistic, just tell them that the more people concentrate on this stuff, the more it will happen. The more they discuss it, the more they will manifest it. Say you don't want to be responsible for that, and ask if they do. You never know, you might be their angel that day. This is a very good resolution to make.

CHANGE THE WORLD FOR ONE PERSON

Lots of people will try and put you down by saying one person cannot change the world. Resolve to tell them that you're changing the world one person at a time. One person may not be able to change the world, but they can change the world for one person. Resolve to do good deeds without payment or favours and in doing so you'll change that person's world. If everyone did this every day, then before long the whole world *could* be changed.

February Angels

The weather outside is almost always cold and wet at this time of year, so snuggle up cozily indoors with angelic energy in the form of candles, open fires and loved ones. Flames and angels always seem to go well together, I think, and this month's angel is Barchiel. If you happen to have been born in this month, like me, this angel is known as one to help you attain patience. I know that patience is what I'm here to learn in this lifetime! February can tend to make it seem like winter is dragging out and we long for spring and warm, sunny days. Try instead to appreciate the beauty of snow and rejoice that we have such a varied climate instead of it always being the same. In the garden you can almost feel the trees and grass trembling with life in anticipation of the blooming to come, and your year can be just the same.

HOLD ON TO THE PROMISE

In February things are full of promise in one respect, in that spring is just around the corner, but also, if the winter's been long and hard, it can be a depressing time of year. February can also bring a resumption of very cold weather, even heavy snow, and it can be the last straw at the end of a demanding winter. A lot of people even suffer from SAD (Seasonal Affective Disorder), which is basically a need for more natural light and more sunshine. Your angels can help with this, and at the end of this chapter I've created a special meditation to give you a starting point.

Today Tony and I had to drive into town through a countryside that barely made it above –4° all day. The fields were whited out and it was really awfully cold. But once we started to notice the beauty of the glittering white, frost-encrusted tree sculptures, and we realized that we were driving through what looked like the film set for *The Chronicles of Narnia*, we were overtaken by admiration and forgot about the cold.

At this time of year children can feel a bit low, too, and sometimes this can make them get up to mischief from which they need rescuing. Christmas has gone and for them an anti-climax can start to be felt. I was told this amazing story about just such a child and his rather unexpected rescuer.

Gordon's Story

The freezer warehouse was the biggest shop I've ever seen. We're going back a few years now to when I was a stripling of a mere 80 years of age. I'm 97 now. In those days freezers were, I believe, heavier than they are now. I was watching this young lad running riot through the place, opening and slamming lids on freezers and taking no notice of his mum's shouting or the salespeople's dirty looks. Luckily, there were only two of them around, it being close to lunch-time. I was thinking about buying a small freezer – not one of the mammoth ones; no point with there just being me at home. Anyway, it seems that the kid's parents finally made a choice and were ushered away into the office to sign the papers or whatever. The kid, one salesgirl down the other end and I were the only ones left. I guess the parents thought their child couldn't do much harm to all those boxes – he was only about four years old anyway – and maybe they relished his being out of their way for a bit in what, to him, was a huge playground. Next thing I knew, I heard a loud and terrified yell from the salesgirl. I turned and looked, and she was pointing about halfway down the store. I don't know how it happened but it seems a stand had given way on one corner, and the precariously balanced chest freezer on it had toppled over. The boy was trapped underneath it. I ran for it. I hadn't run in years, but now I did, sprinting down the aisle and beating the girl there. The little lad was pinned on his back with the freezer across his tummy. I could hear voices, as I think the parents were shouting something, asking what was wrong, but they couldn't see from where they were. I reached down with both hands and hauled at the freezer. It wouldn't budge, of course. I looked heavenwards and yelled, 'Help me!' I grabbed the freezer again and, to my constant and everlasting amazement, the freezer seemed to suddenly weigh just a few pounds. I lifted it up and off the boy and stood it on the floor. Then I fell over. I sat there panting as the lad jumped up, unharmed, just in time for a rollocking from his mum and dad. The salesgirl stood there, mouth open in astonishment at what she'd seen me do, but really everyone else was thinking about the boy. I'm guessing the parents were wondering if they were going to have to pay for the freezer, and the manager, who by then had heard the screams and come running, was wondering if he was going to be sued.

Me? I was just wondering what exactly had given me that temporary strength...

Gordon was given the strength by his angel, who is called *Hulama*, which means 'rising up' in Hawaiian. This angel gave Gordon the power of several men for that moment, both to save the child and to give him confidence in his own immortality – something he needed at that time. This sort of phenomenon has been recorded many times in the media, such as when people are suddenly able to force open burning car doors or even lift a car off someone who is trapped beneath.

Holly's Story

When I was a teenager I had a bad accident. I'd become really, really angry about something and I smashed my fist into a shed window. The glass shattered and sliced into my arm. There was such a lot of blood suddenly. It turned out the glass had severed my main artery in my wrist as well as three tendons, and I lost over 50 per cent of my blood before they could stop it. I had to have emergency micro-surgery, and I actually died twice during the operation. During this time I could see my body lying on the bed, with doctors running around me. I heard two of the nurses suggesting that I'd done it on purpose to self-harm, but that wasn't the case. I seemed to be looking down on myself, and I could even see the blood transfusion bags hooked up to my feet, and I wondered how I could see that if I was lying down. But the weirdest part was that my sister Belinda was there holding my hand, and saying, 'You're not going anywhere!' over and over while squeezing my hand. When I finally came to, my family was in the hospital room but I couldn't see Belinda, so I asked, 'Where's Bel? She was there holding my hand in surgery.'

My older sister Narelle said, 'No. Bel hasn't been here yet. She stayed at home, keeping Dad up to date.' My dad was in Alice Springs, although of course as soon as he heard what had happened he'd jumped into the car and driven to Adelaide, arriving at my bedside within 14 hours. When I told Bel what I'd seen while I was 'dead', she said, 'I was at home praying, and saying, "You're not going anywhere."'

Even today we still speak of how Bel was there with me. This experience taught me a valuable lesson, and it also made me who I am today.

This is a classic tale of an angel giving a stern lesson in not losing patience and in curbing your temper. This experience showed Holly several things: that anger hurts mostly those who feel it rather than the person against whom it's directed (literally and figuratively in this case!); that her angel was watching over her (and, in being shown herself from the outside, from her angel's viewpoint, how to see herself more clearly); that her sister's energy could be with her wherever they physically were, as anyone's can; and that there is life after death. All in all, a truly amazing experience.

Michelle's Story

It was a freezing February morning and I was out walking the dogs over the fields, which were covered in a heavy frost. The next day my partner and I were due to fly to Cuba on our own, leaving behind my son, Sam, who was then 11. He would be staying with friends. I suddenly had a wave of negative energy – comprising of guilt and regret that he wasn't coming with us, and the usual maternal panic about what might happen while I was apart from my child.

My intuitive voice was telling me not to worry and that everything would be fine. I then was led to look up to the grey sky, when out of nowhere there appeared a beautiful white feather which softly fell, moving side to side, just in front of me.

I knew this was a message from my guardian angel to reassure me that all would be well and that I should go on my holiday leaving behind the negative energy. I felt overwhelmed with love and relief. Of course Sam enjoyed his time with our friends, and we had a lovely holiday. In fact we all enjoyed a bit of healthy space that was much needed.

STRATEGIES FOR FEBRUARY
LET THE SUNSHINE IN!

To get some angelic substitute for sunshine's vitamin D, first find yourself a south-facing area. I always enjoy it better if I can sit on a south-facing slope, which has the added benefit of providing some shelter from cold north winds. This works best, of course, if it's a sunny day, but angels can still bring in solar energy through the clouds, if you ask them to. So, having wrapped up warm and sought out the best spot, close your eyes and concentrate on the colours of yellow and orange. Ask your angels to take up these colours and come to you from the south. Concentrate on your inner eyelids, and after a few seconds you should start to sense light building in front of your closed eyes and penetrating your eyelids. Feel this brightness envelop your whole body, until you don't feel the cold at all. Allow your body to absorb this 'alternative sunshine' through your skin, until your very bones feel bathed in it. This treatment will give you a huge boost.

STAINS OF WONDER

One of the best things I ever bought for our house was a stained glass window for the front door. It's made even better by the fact that Tony and I designed it ourselves, because when you make something, you naturally connect it to your own energy. If the winter is seeming to drag on too long, on a sunny day the coloured lights on the hall wall created by the panels of red, blue and amber glass in the door light up the room, doubling or even trebling the power of the weak sunlight. Just standing there, leaning on the wall, allows me to bathe in the coloured light, and it never fails to uplift my spirit. Of course not everyone is able to have a whole stained glass window of their choice, so for an easier, cheaper option, you can just get some small, different coloured glass panels and hang them in the sunlight, choosing whichever colour suits your mood that day.

You should start off with the colours you think you'll need most, to keep costs down, and gradually add to them. I've been using coloured light for a while, and these are the pointers I've come up with:

- Turquoise – opens the mind and soul to new experiences. If change is a worry, this light will help.

- Red – empowers and energizes. If you've been feeling a bit below par, this will help.

- Yellow – the sunshine colour, which will give you a lot of the same things you get from a suntan, like a feeling of wellbeing and the ability to have fun.

- Blue – will calm you down and stop you panicking about insignificant stuff.

- Orange – will give you courage to face tougher challenges and also help you make decisions, such as whether to move house.

- Indigo or violet – will encourage soul connection and help enhance intuition.

- Green – will help heal you and bring about resolution that has been elusive.

- Pink – will help you feel less alone and more deserving of the unconditional love your angels feel for you.

SEE BEAUTY IN THE COLD

February can bring you down if the cold weather grabs tight and the frost doesn't melt all day. But try and see beauty in it. We were out for a walk the other day, taking photos of the very thick frost. Ice crystals are one of the most amazing of Nature's beauties. It never fails to amaze me how intricate, delicate and magical they are. Being amazed is a very good way of creating the right sort of energy for angel connection. Recently, we had the most frost I've ever seen. Today the sky turned baby blue and I've never seen anything so magical as the fronds and twigs of the trees with a backdrop of palest blue. When lit by the low sun, sideways, they took my breath away. Then as the sun set and the sky turned pink, the ice reflected the colour, turning the whole world rosy. I know that at these moments angels are around me. Try this sort of thing for yourself.

VALENTINE'S DAY

I couldn't leave this month without a nod to romantic Valentine's Day, which can hold a promise of a different kind. Once you've met your soulmate, or if you already have met them, what kind of Valentine's Day celebration will enhance your connections to your angels and multiply your chances of 'happily ever after'? Give your lover the greatest gift: time. Switch off the mobile phone and the TV and create a special sanctuary for the two of you to share. Use fairy-lights in abundance and drape fancy fabrics like silk and velvet over the seating. Light as many candles as you can to create a soft atmosphere, and lay a table with food you know your partner loves. Making the evening all about them will be the greatest act of love. Love is a very positive emotion and by creating this perfect demonstration of unconditional love, you'll attract angel energy to you both.

March Angels

In the early springtime, animals and birds get together to produce babies, and knowing how quickly the seasons can turn, they want to get ahead. The angel for this month is Machidiel, who encourages us to consider breaking fresh ground and generating the energy necessary to give our longed-for reality a kickstart. If your wish is for a child of your own but you're having difficulties conceiving, then this angel is capable of lighting the way forward. If convention hasn't produced your desired result, this angel will help you think laterally and be open enough and courageous enough to consider new approaches.

THINGS CAN GO RIGHT IF YOU THINK LATERALLY

From the letters I receive, the most common problem at this time is from couples who don't seem to be able to conceive a baby, despite passing all the regular health and fertility checks that are available. In some cases, when help is asked for, it might come in an unusual or unexpected form, but I always ask people who doubt, 'What have you got to lose by trying?'

People tend not to want their real names published for this kind of story, but I have some very brief anecdotes from people whose angels have given them advice.

Tracey's Story

After three miscarriages we decided to follow Jenny's advice and have our hair analysed, which had seemed a freaky idea up until then. Following it, I was told to take certain vitamins. After just one month of trying, I was pregnant!

Jayne's Story

After many miscarriages, even after getting successfully pregnant following IVF treatment, I persuaded my husband, who was very doubtful, to contact a company called Foresight. This advice was given to me by a psychic, which is why my hubby was doubtful! But they told me that I had too much mercury in my system from eating things like contaminated tinned fish, which is polluted. We undertook a special course to clear my system, and less than a month later I was pregnant with our adorable daughter, who is now one year old.

WHEN THINGS GO WRONG

Sometimes things do go wrong, and people have to try and find a way to deal with that. Teresa sent me a story of what I call 'the baby angel'. Over the years many mums have written to me about this being. He seems to come in all shapes and sizes, but the stories are similar enough that it's obvious there's a strong pattern. So much so that I honestly believe there is a special angel who comes to collect babies who have died. I also believe that these babies are taken straight to those parts of their parents which reside permanently in spirit, and so they are never alone and never really separated from their parents.

I had a son who was born 15 weeks early after an unexpected pregnancy. I already had a daughter who was just a few months old when I discovered I was pregnant again, and I knew having another child so soon was going to be tough but I got used to the idea. I was scared of labour, having had such a painful time before, and I had still only just turned 18. I went into early labour on 21 March 2000, and when my son was born at 4:30 p.m. he was fighting for his life right away, because he was 15 weeks early. He only weighed 1lb 5oz, and I called him Paul. I prayed to God to let him live. Watching my little boy fight for his first few months of life made me feel so helpless. I had instant, unconditional love for this child and couldn't wait to be allowed to take him home, and that day finally came on 16 July 2000. I thought that finally the battle was over and I could enjoy this life and move forward.

Both of my children made me very happy, so that I looked forward to the morning and seeing them. Because Paul was born early, he had a few medical conditions and had to visit the doctor often, mainly weekly. Eventually, the doctor told me that she was very happy with him and wouldn't have to see him so often. Paul's first birthday was coming up by then, and I felt confident enough to let my guard down and to stop worrying every day. The doctor's words made me feel that everything was going to be all right. Of course my little man might have been small for his age, but he sure did have a big heart and he was strong.

But on 21 April 2001, my life came to a standstill when my baby Paul passed away, leaving me in a world of sadness. I didn't know what to do, as I didn't feel I had anything to live for, even though Lucy was soon to turn two years old and I knew I had to carry on for her. I wanted to keep busy so not long afterwards I went to college to study childcare. It was the skill I was good at. From time to time I get sad and think of Paul. It gets too much sometimes, and then I hide away in my home and don't answer to people. One night, a couple of years after he'd passed away, when I'd shut myself off from the world and was clinging to my grief for Paul, I heard a noise. Rachel, the other little girl I had by then, was lying across my leg, and Lucy was in the bed with us as well. I had cramp in my leg from Rachel's weight and I looked up to see where the noise was coming from. I could see a little kid playing with the children's kitchen set. I nearly had a heart attack, and then I remembered something from before Paul had died. I had seen a man with long curly hair and bright, sky-blue eyes and a long face in my house. Of course that man didn't say a word to me and I don't know how he got in because the door was locked, as I didn't like people walking in without knocking. I knew at that second that I was now seeing my son again, and I was no longer scared, only sad because I knew I couldn't have him in my arms again...

Teresa's story appears to have a sad ending in that Paul has gone. However, I've also received enough of the kinds of stories that follow to make me think that all hope for him coming back is not gone. I have a firm belief that no souls are ever wasted, and babies who have a struggle making it into our lives are often rehearsing, making stronger and stronger connections with their mothers until that connection is so strong that it can withstand anything and make it through to life. When babies do pass away, stories like Teresa's bring some comfort in that at least those little souls are being taken care of by their very own angel.

Caroline's Story

I'd lost five pregnancies, and they were the worst kind. They were the kind where the baby had died inside me and had to be removed. There were no sadder moments in my life than when I had to sit in a ward of women with live babies inside them, waiting for mine to be washed away like unwanted rubbish. This happened many years ago, and I understand things are done a little more sensitively nowadays. Anyway, we'd tried everything. I'd had stitches to hold the baby in place. I'd spent weeks scooting around everywhere on my butt, not daring to stand erect or walk anywhere for fear of triggering a problem, but nothing worked and the babies died. So, having tried everything and having only surrogacy left to try (which was practically unheard of in those days), I felt I was never going to be a mother or give my husband his longed-for son. Then I met a remarkable woman. She told me that she could 'see' I'd had past-life problems and that all I needed to do, in my case, was to resolve those issues; then, if I was ever meant to have a child, I would. I have to confess I didn't really believe her at the time and thought I had enough 'real' problems in this life without stirring up old issues that may or may not be real. But I guess my angels heard my cries for help somewhere along the line, because they took things in hand.

I had a dream. I saw myself as a raggedly dressed woman, I think on the streets of Victorian London. There were horses and carriages and people dressed in those kinds of clothes. I felt like I was sort of floating above myself (I was told later that I might have been doing what they call 'astral travelling', where you go somewhere else in time and place in a sort of real dream). In this dream I had two snotty-nosed kids with me, both boys. They were dressed in rags, too, and it was cold, freezing. I could see all the breath clouding white from their mouths. The boys were crying, hungry, begging their mother (me) for food, but she didn't have any. I couldn't believe how people were just passing them by, not caring. No one even looked at them, and it was as if they were invisible. No one seemed to see me either where I drifted above the scene. I remember thinking how great it was not to live in those times. It was obvious that the three of them were dying and in 'my' time, today, there was help for people like that. I felt that the world had learned to care a bit more than it used to about poor people. I remember thinking how glad I was to live in the Western world, where the state helps us, and with that thought I woke up.

I realized straight away that this had been more than a dream and I felt that my angels had taken me back to my past, not to suffer, but to realize that things were different now. I went back to sleep and had another dream. This time I saw an angel and it spoke to me. It told me that I'd been subconsciously telling my body to let my babies go because I was afraid I wouldn't be able to take care of them, just as I hadn't back in the past life I'd seen. The angel told me that if I let that past go and understood that I had plenty of safety nets in this life, things would change. By the next morning I felt very optimistic and a weight had lifted from me. Enough to say that today I have two grown-up sons, and I believe they are the same boys I lost back in Victorian England. I also believe they are the same souls that I lost five times and would have gone on losing if my angels hadn't helped me.

I have been given a name for the 'baby angel'. It is *Mayura*, which is a Sanskrit word for a peacock. Peacocks are symbols of great integrity, so mothers who lose a child can certainly trust this angel to bring their babies home.

STRATEGIES FOR MARCH
DREAM TIME AND ASTRAL TRAVEL

Astral travel is a great way to connect with your angels to ask them for help, no matter what area in your life needs it most. There's a special time during the night, between 3 and 5 a.m., when a lot of people wake up and can't get back to sleep. More and more people are telling me this is happening to them. I believe it's to do with our rapid approach to 2012, when the spirituality of the world is due to change. This wake-up is a sort of soul alarm, telling the person that the time is right for some astral travel. So, next time this happens to you, instead of moaning, take advantage of it! The easiest way to set off is to count your breaths backwards from 200. At some point you'll feel yourself drifting, not quite asleep, and this is the moment to tell your angel to take you to where or when you need to go. Or, if that doesn't happen spontaneously, while counting backwards, picture a silver cord running from your head to the ceiling and through it. Make the cord so real that you feel if you reached up you could actually touch it. Once you're convinced it's real, then see yourself rising up it. Not your physical body, but a ghost-like form of yourself, weightless and able to rise effortlessly up the cord. Also, allow your mind to run free at this point and take you wherever your angel leads. It is possible that your angel can introduce you to your future child while you're travelling.

THE CHILD IN YOU

One way to change your own energy to make it more compatible with that of a child is to re-welcome your own inner child. Think back to a time as a child when perhaps you were feeling a little sad. Perhaps you'd been told off and felt guilty, or a friend had snubbed you, or a pet had died. Picture yourself standing in front of the child you were at that sad time and as the adult you are now, think of the right words to comfort that child. Speak the words out loud and tell the child that you will be their angel for the day. Put your arms around the child and draw them back into your current body, telling them you welcome them and you'll always protect them.

NO WEEDS HERE

Your body, when you're trying for a child, can be likened to a garden. It's all very well planting seeds in a garden, but unless the environment is right, the seeds won't grow and the plant will fade and die. In meditation, ask your angels to tell you what you need to eat, how you need to exercise and what state of mind you need in order to create the very best possible environment for the child you're hoping to create. If your body is too acidic an embryo cannot survive there, so ask your angels to give you an intuitive feel for when you need to alkalize your body and keep it in balance. Your angels will be better able to help you if you can be specific like this about what you need from them.

April Angels

Now is the time to spring-clean your house, your energetic frequency and even your whole life, with a little help from the angels. The one to help you achieve this is Asmodel. This April angel will help you get rid of outmoded, self-destructive behaviour and forge ahead into new areas and thought processes. It may be that past lives are still affecting your progress in this current life, and this angel will be very useful in sweeping the past away and showing you that the future can be just as exciting as you always hoped it would. April and Asmodel are both associated with re-birth, so this is your time to take steps into the future with fresh energy.

GET MOVING

Because of this month's fresh appeal, it's a good time to move house as well, but sometimes you can get stuck: your house won't sell, your energy slumps and things look hopeless. John and Bev Page had a reading done by me in my *Take 5* column in Australia. They were stuck in a house in which they no longer felt at home and were having trouble selling. The house was a lovely big family home, but needed the right buyers. They needed to be people who wanted a big house but didn't have the funds to buy one in top condition. Bev and John had been married for 45 years and had always believed in their angels. They wanted to know the names of their angels, though, and I was able to help them with this and give them reassurance that all would be OK with their home. I told them what signs to watch for and how to know when the timing was right for a big push.

Recently, they sent me an email updating me on their progress:

Don't know if you'll remember us – Bev and John Page from Sydney, Australia. We contacted you and had an aura reading done through *Take 5* magazine. One of the questions we asked was whether we'd be able to sell our dilapidated house and buy a new one. Our angels looked after us beautifully, just as you said, and it all fell into place. I won't go into all the details as it is too long a story and would bore you silly, but our house sold in three days to a lovely young couple with three little girls (and they want a fourth child) and this house, although dilapidated, has five bedrooms and two bathrooms, and the rooms are quite large. They weren't ready to buy and we weren't ready to sell but we had put a sign 'expressions of interest invited' – and they drove past, and then came through. They loved the old house, loved the very large block of land and decided to buy it and renovate. Amazing! We have been looking for a house to buy, couldn't afford anything in the area we wanted, so we started looking elsewhere. We went to an open house at 10 a.m. this day, but the house just wasn't right. We had another appointment for 1:30, so we decided to just drive around the area to see if we liked it. In the same street was another house which took my eye, but we'd seen it on the net and couldn't work out why we'd rejected it. I took the name of the agent and the phone number, asked John if we could ring up and see if there was going to be a viewing that day while we were in the area. He wasn't keen but I pushed, so we did, and the agent said we could come and look at it with another couple. We looked, we really liked it and went away to discuss it. We asked the agent if she was working the next day and if we could bring our daughters with us to get another opinion. The long and short of it was: our daughter and her eldest son came with us, loved the house, we went away and talked about it, made an offer, the agent got back to us with their counter-offer and we accepted! We put down the holding deposit (until we could get the building and pest inspections done) on our son Scott's birthday (he passed away 15 years ago this month). Also, these people have a picture of angels behind their bed, so all the signs were there that you told us to watch for.

We believe our angels were all looking after us, especially Scott. Lovely story, isn't it? We're very excited about the whole thing and can't wait to move into our beautiful new home. It's also lovely that our old house is not going to be pulled down after all, and these young people are going to make it lovely again and it will have little children laughing and playing in it once more.

The rather sad epilogue to this story is that the couple were due to move house in November 2010, but the sale was brought forward (most unusually) to September 2010. John had been ill for some time but then died very unexpectedly after spending just nine days in their dream house. Bev sensed angel intervention again, and I'm sure she's right. If the sale had been completed on the original date, John would never have lived there. Not only did the angels know how important it was for him to get into the house, but also how very important it was for Bev that her beloved John was at least in the house with her, now that she is there alone. It would have been awful if she'd had to move there on her own after he'd passed away, leaving all the memories of him behind in the old house. Bev has become a dear friend, as have many of my *Take 5* readers, and I look forward to staying in touch with her.

This was the message I was able to give her from John:

Never save things for 'best', but enjoy your treasures every day. A smile, a touch of the hand. Give these things and, in turn, receive them. Real love never truly dies, it just changes form.

Apparently, John is going to come to you at times of 'play'. He'll be with you more at those times than he's been able to be for a while.

He says to relax, and that there is a surprise coming in the near future, which he has arranged. The whole family will be involved in this celebration.

I keep getting a sense of wonder from John – it's like, 'Oh, I *see*! Now I understand!' He seems to be enjoying himself, and I think I know why.

I don't know if you know, but many people, including me, believe that we all keep a part of us in spirit all the time – in fact, our greater part. The part of us that gets snipped off and goes to the Earth plane in a mortal body is actually quite a small part of all we are.

I think John has just discovered this and is overjoyed to have been reunited with *his* greater part, but not only that; he is also reunited with *your* greatest part, and also your *son*, Scott's.

So, you see, although it's tough for you to be alone down here, every time you connect with your own spirit and soul, you connect with them, too. And even should either of them decide to be 'snipped' and come back to Earth before you leave it, it won't matter, because their greater parts will still be waiting for you 'over there'.

Bev's angel and the one that made the story possible is called *Kakumulani*, which means 'the horizon' in Hawaiian. This is the place where her dear John waits for her and where she'll be able to sense him every sunrise and sunset.

NEW HORIZONS TAILOR-MADE FOR YOU

I recently did a reading for a young woman in my *Soul & Spirit* column, which changed everything for her.

This was her letter:

Dear Jenny,

I have had a difficult few years and have slowly been recovering from ME, which has kind of put my life on hold. In the last two years I have been able to do more and have started to do a little part-time healing work from home. I have been stuck for so long it is sometimes hard to feel that it ever will change and get better, but in the last week I have felt my angel around me a lot, really closely. It feels like she has been giving me lots of healing. I get the name *Sariel*? I am feeling much more positive and think I am finally ready to move forward and be well again. I really want to but am scared to fully believe it and be disappointed again. Am I really going forward now? And is the healing and teaching Reiki still the right path for me to take? There has been so much change going on that it has left me a little shaken up!

Thank you so much. I love your angel Q&A every month, your energy and guidance, and the pictures are always beautiful.

Sarah

And here's my reply:

Dear Sarah,

It's rare that I get such exciting news to pass on! Your name for your angel is spot on, and it means 'Command from God' in Aramaic. You are certainly receiving your 'orders' because your communication is very good indeed! There is some important advice for you: you are to begin a whole new healing modality. Your angel is attuned to crystals, and this is what you are to do, too. Your new modality is a 'new take' on hot stone massage and Reiki combined. You are to take tumble stones, chosen by you individually for each client, and warm them gently in a herbal heat pack (heated by microwave). The particular herbs will also be chosen by you for each client. Then use them to massage as is normally done in hot stone massage. This way you'll impart your healing through the warm crystals, thus enhancing both your and their healing abilities, while at the same time the client will be enveloped in the healing aromas of the warm herbs. You will create a little medicine sack for each client to take home, which will include a spray of the herb used and two of the tumble stones used. Your angel assures me that this combination will be totally original to you and you must name it and copyright it immediately after reading this message, and put it on a website to protect it as yours. Make sure that anyone else using it has to be accredited by you. You will go on to write articles for magazines in this new modality and become very well known as the creator of it.

The other thing you need to cultivate in your life is a sense of teamwork, and as you teach people and as your healing centre grows, this will all come quite naturally. Congratulations, Sarah, your future is going to be very exciting indeed.

An update:

> Thank you so much – I am so excited! The reading was
> amazing and my angel picture is beautiful. I love it.
> Thanks, Jenny, for the reading and for being so helpful. I
> will definitely be trying the advice. I knew I needed to do
> something but couldn't quite work it out, so it is fantastic
> to have such clear guidance. I will let you know as soon
> as I am up and running. It might take a while to set up and
> get going but I will get started straight away so hopefully
> it won't be long!
>
> Thanks again
>
> *Sarah*

Sarah did indeed take all this advice on board and I've
included her new website in the Resources chapter; if you
visit the site you can also see the portrait of Sariel that I
created for her.

STRATEGIES FOR APRIL
HUG THAT TREE!

This is a good time to start tree-hugging if you've never
done it before. The reason for this is that trees in April are
gathering themselves for a surge into spring. That means
their energy can be felt much more easily at this time, as

it's more powerful. People who've maybe laughed at the idea of connecting with a tree can be greatly surprised if they just try it. First of all, get yourself acclimatized by initially hugging trees that are healthy and vital, and then compare that with a hug given to a poorly, dried-out tree. This is the way to really start believing that you can sense a tree's energy. The difference between the two is unmistakable. Once you've let go of logic and allowed yourself to 'sink' into a tree's energy, you'll start to feel it pulsing up beneath the bark, like a river. This connection to the universe can only bring you closer to angels, and during a tree-hug is a good time to ask for help.

GOD'S GLORY

Angels are our go-betweens. Without them we wouldn't always be able to connect to God, to the Supreme Master of the universe. People who know me know that, to me, 'God' is another name for our intelligent universe, but whatever you call the creator, it doesn't matter. The thing is, we all need to see angels everywhere, every day. In spring we're surrounded by beech trees, which to me are the most beautiful of our native British trees. They are always providing me with uplifting sights. In spring it's the way the sunlight filters in dapples through the young, acid-green leaves. It's the way the branches fall in graceful arches, like a fanned umbrella. At this time of year, beneath them are clouds of native bluebells, with colour so intense that they seem to turn the very air indigo. I would say that my most favourite natural sight in the world is a clearing in the beech wood that is filled with nodding heads of these incredibly beautiful flowers. With sights like this in front of you it's almost impossible not to find yourself in the company of angels.

NEW IN THE MOON

The moon and moonlight are powerful energy-creators. There is a unique energy available to us all in the white light from this celestial friend. This technique requires that you have a private outside area, because the first thing you need to do is take off all your clothes. It can work if you're clothed, but it won't give you as much. Then simply stand in the moonlight. Obviously, a full moon is best, but any time is good. Turn round and round with your arms raised so that every part of you is bathed in the magical light of the moon's rays. Close your eyes and you'll find it's also easy at this point to imagine your angel standing right in front of you, perhaps in a gown that glistens and sparkles in the moonlight. The more detail you can imagine, the more effective this will be.

May Angels

Now is the time to get outdoors with the wildflowers that abound in this month in the UK, and rejoice at all the blossom. Connecting with your angel at this time can give you an opportunity to do so with renewed energy, by connecting with them through the planet. To help you in this you can call on this month's angel, Ambriel. This angel is the one who will protect your endeavours. Ambriel will also guide you to be able to see the real truth and understand who you really are deep inside. There can be no pretence in the presence of this angel, so open your heart to your inner truth and, from this position of knowledge, your path will become clear.

MAGICAL MAY

Lots of readers seem to have angelic experiences around this time of year, and May is my favourite month because many things happened to me at this special time. I met my past-life husband, Garth Brooks, in May. I got the first good contract for a book I'd written in May. Spring is the time to start new quests, and I was recently at Quest, the massive Devon-based healing festival – a date which had been offered and confirmed in the previous May. While I was there, two very special things happened: I met Michelle Corrigan, a fellow light-worker and author, and we were like old friends instantly. Also, two readers of my *Take 5* column in Australia, Liz and Kevin, were in the UK at the time and travelled to Quest specifically to meet me, which was lovely.

Michelle told me of some wonderful experiences she'd had that turned her life upside-down.

> I was suffering with dreadful menstrual problems which included terrible pain, heavy bleeding and vomiting during my periods. After some hospital tests, I received a letter saying that I had an ovarian cyst on the right side and would need treatment, which made my heart sink as I have a real fear of hospitals and any medical equipment coming near me. I received several sessions of spiritual healing from a fabulous lady who works with angels and spirit guides to channel the healing energy. I also did self-healing, asking the angels to take away the cyst so I wouldn't need any hospital treatment.
>
> One night after a particular powerful healing session, in my bedroom I saw a vision of a beautiful angel, which

brought with it the most incredible energy of softness and beauty. The next thing I knew, I suddenly needed to pee quite badly. I went to the bathroom and suddenly felt quite a sharp pain in the right side of my groin, which felt as if I was having my period, but that wasn't actually due. I turned the light on and looked in the toilet and saw a mass that I can only describe as a tumour, which I had obviously passed.

I spent the next day resting and healing, and after that I haven't looked back. Along with the angel healing, yoga, homoeopathic remedies and self-development, I feel absolutely brilliant, have no menstrual problems and have now entered my menopause naturally without trying to suppress the symptoms with medication such as HRT.

Once when I was visiting my elderly father, I suddenly felt a sharp pain in my heart along with nausea and dizziness. My father was sitting in his chair and looked as if he was at death's door. I rushed over to him and asked him what was wrong. He replied that his heart didn't feel right; he felt sick and dizzy and then he went a bit incoherent, not recognizing other members of the family who were there.

I placed my hands on his shoulders and prayed to the angels to send him healing. In my mind I saw a beautiful healing purple energy and saw the guardian angel who was sending my dad angelic healing, which was going to where it was needed and for his higher good.

Twenty minutes later my dad was drinking a cup of tea and was chatting normally, as if nothing had occurred. I gave my thanks to the angels and knew that it wasn't yet my dad's time to pass over to spirit.

Michelle's guardian angel's name has been channelled in another chapter, which features another of her experiences. I also had a surprising visit while I was at the Quest festival. A wonderful Australian couple I'd met through doing a reading for them in *Take 5* magazine emailed me to say they were going to be in Devon at the time and could they come to see me at my home? The problem was that I wasn't going to be there – I was going to be at Quest on the day they'd chosen. But of course synchronicity stepped in, because Quest is in Devon. So the friends, Kevin and Liz, were able to seek me out at Quest and spend some time with me, which was lovely.

Another reader, Kathleen, told me her story of a spring awakening.

Many years ago I inherited the old school piano. I've never been taught to play the piano and I can't play properly, but for some unknown reason I sat down and my fingers began to play this piece of beautiful music. It's called 'Meditative Pachelbel with Ocean' [a reworking of Pachelbel's Canon in D major]. The tune just came as my fingers touched the keys. I didn't play it well but I still found myself playing it. Since then, whenever I go into garden centres it will be playing. It's so beautiful and makes me feel overwhelmed and spiritual. I do believe that someone's watching over me when I hear this.

Kathleen's angel gave me the name *Harue*, which is Japanese for a 'loving blessing'. This is what music is to her. She'll find it's always easier to connect to her angels with the right kind of music playing.

Linda told me her story of a strange happening where her angels rejuvenated her energy with a wonderful sign that she and her children were being looked after.

Quite a few years ago I was a single parent, struggling to bring up three children. It was a tough time. I was always tired, and this particular night was no exception. I finally got all the kids to bed and was able to relax for a while. But I was too tired to enjoy TV or read, so I decided I'd go to bed, too. I expected to be out like a light as soon as my head hit the pillow, but it wasn't to be. You know how it is when something's preying on your mind and it's almost like dreaming? You know there's something you just have to do before you can really relax, but you're so physically tired it's hard to make yourself get up and do it. All that kept running through my mind was that I needed to get up and pull the TV plug out of the socket. Something wasn't going to let me sleep until I did it. I resisted for a while, telling myself I'd never bothered before so why did my mind keep me awake about it now? Anyway, in the end I got up, went back to the sitting room and unplugged the TV. *There*, I thought, *now can I sleep!* I went straight to sleep as soon as I got into bed and didn't stir until morning. The TV always got put on by the kids, so when I got up, the first thing I did was put the plug back in the wall socket. As I did, there was an almighty bang as the fuse blew. I really do feel that my guardian angel made me get up and unplug the TV, and if I hadn't listened and done it, we could have been caught in a fire.

Linda's angel has given me the name *Chou*, which means 'butterfly' in Japanese. This is to let Linda know that her angel is always around and that she's never really alone. It's also to remind her that in time she emerged into her own light and life, just like a butterfly emerges from a chrysalis.

Some readers of my *Take 5* column in Australia wrote me an interesting letter that demonstrates how easy it can be to misinterpret an angelic message. This will of course happen more often if the people involved have a tendency to be a bit negative. It's easy to miss a positive message if you're feeling a bit low or down for whatever reason. It's sad that sometimes angels have done their best to uplift us only to find that in fact they've made us feel worse because we haven't understood the message. Because this is all down to our own energy state, it sometimes means we miss out on their help just when we most need it.

We think we're being haunted, but by someone who's alive! It's as if we're hexed by Celine Dion. It started about ten years ago when our beloved dog, Holly, who'd been on chemotherapy for 13 months, had to be released from her agony at last. The vet came to our home and put her to sleep on the couch. Just at the moment when Holly's eyes met ours, so trustingly, for the last time, the kitchen radio started playing, 'My Heart Will Go On', sung by Celine Dion. We thought it was a very sad coincidence that this should be playing just as our dear dog was dying. Ten years passed without any problems, and then it happened again. Our other dog had reached the end. She had kidney problems and was at the vet's on a drip. The next morning the vet phoned to tell us that we needed to go in to say our goodbyes. Then, just as Amber had the deadly injection, the radio at the vet's played the exact same song, 'My Heart Will Go On'. We were totally heartbroken. Why is this happening to my family?

Of course what was actually happening was that the wonderful dogs were held by angels as they died and were able to send this message through the words of the song. Their lives were not over and their immortal souls will go on for ever. It was actually a wonderful message of comfort and joy, rather than some sort of hex.

I've been given the name *Chamanit* for this family, which means 'golden flower' in Hebrew. This is how their dogs want to be remembered, as beautiful bright flowers that grow and blossom, but then fade in time – only to be renewed as their seeds grow again. The dogs never really died and will be coming back.

Terry Ann shared this wonderful experience with me.

We moved to New Mexico from Florida for my husband's work. We bought a home in Rio Rancho, a suburb of Albuquerque. Two weeks after we bought the home, his work closed the doors and the company for which he worked claimed bankruptcy. He's an aeronautic technician and there was no work in New Mexico, and we knew we would have to move back to the East Coast. He got contract work and lived away from home, and I had to remain behind to sell the home we'd just bought and take care of our dog and three cats. So there I was, living in a new place, holding down the fort, so to speak. It was hard to sell a five-bedroom house in the falling economy without losing too much money. About six months went by and my husband was still working away and I was still alone at the house with no bites on the sale. Where we lived is over 5,000 feet above sea level so at night I often lay on the lounge chair and stared at the night sky, which seemed so close. One night while lying out, I just broke down and cried and looked to the universe for help or a sign. I felt like I was only out there for a short time, but in actuality it turned out to be hours.

The next morning my cats were looking out of the glass sliding doors into the enclosed porch. It looked like their attention was caught by a leaf. I walked out and I saw that it was a hummingbird, just sitting there, and it was still alive. It must have gotten trapped in our porch. I picked it up with my hands and brought it inside. I had no idea what to give it since I was in a panic and didn't want it to die. I put some water in my other hand and it drank from my hand. I'd never seen a hummingbird so close in my entire life, and now I was actually holding one. Its long beak had a small tongue, smaller than a toothpick, and I saw it as it was drinking. Then the bird started to flutter its wings, so I went out front, since there were some rose bushes there, and set it on one of the rose bushes. In a few minutes it flew away.

I knew right away that it was a sign to me that everything would be OK and that I should leave, and that I would be helped to fly away. I confidently started to finish packing, and within three days we sold our home to a family who had eight children, for the price we were asking. For days afterwards when I was out walking my dog, a hummingbird would come up to us. I almost expected it. We closed on the house within 30 days. Somehow that was such a powerful sign to me: that, no matter how bad things can be sometimes, we just need to fly and move forward.

We bought an old Victorian house that is over 100 years old and, needless to say, we have activity here because my cats are always seeing and chasing things. My one cat, Olive, is extremely psychic. Every time I clean my crystal ball she'll just gaze into it. I've had friends over and I'll put down the crystal ball and she'll start gazing every time… it's truly amazing how attracted she is to it…

Well, that is the experience that stands out in my life.

Terry Ann's angel has given me the name *Chronos*, which means 'time' in Greek. This is to remind her that once you have faith, things will slot into place no matter how impossible they may seem – at the right moment. Heaven's time is hard to understand in times of stress, but even angels have to take the time to get things absolutely right for one person, without making them wrong for another.

STRATEGIES FOR MAY
SANCTUARY!

Make plans to create an outdoor sanctuary where you can go to connect to your angels. Creating something like this means that when you enter it, you also enter the right mindset, which is half the battle! This can be anything from a beautiful summerhouse to a humble bench under a tree. The important thing is to create the right ambience for angelic energy and connection to it, so use things you've made yourself if possible. It's not too difficult to make a mosaic from old tiles, perhaps covering the top of an old coffee table. If you then seal it with bathroom grout, the whole thing will be weather-proof. This will not only be something beautiful with your energy all over it, but will be useful for standing candles, crystals and angel statues on.

SITTING DOWN

Of course when you talk to angels, in the house or in your sanctuary, it will help you relax if you can sit comfortably. You can help with this by buying a cheap little stool and then padding the seat and covering it with some sumptuous material, which can be bought from the scrap basket of a fabric store. Choose a good spiritual colour, such as pink or purple. You can add to this as you wish by painting the legs with a pretty colour and adding pictures or stickers of stars, moons and hearts.

WAKING UP

This month, above all others, is to me the right time for waking up spiritually, just as Nature is also leaping into new life. With this in mind, try this really deep meditation.

Imagine you're standing in front of a beautiful lake. The water is shining turquoise in the sunshine, the birds are singing and the reeds are rustling in a soft breeze. Feel the warmth of the sun on your body as you stand beneath a pristine blue sky. Relax, and then relax some more. Ask your angels to bring you fully to life. So many times we feel like we're sleepwalking through a waking dream, and so we don't live in the moment. Tell your angel that you want to start enjoying every second of life and stop waiting for a good thing to happen. Walk forward into the water. Feel its silky coolness in ripples around your ankles. The water isn't cold, just refreshing. Walk forward some more and the water will rise up your body until you're chest deep. Out in the water ahead of you a beautiful angel rises up, and as she sinks again she invites you to join her beneath the surface. With no fear you lift your feet from the pebbly bottom and lower your head into the water. The water doesn't go up your nose and you're able to open your eyes under there. You gently float back up and break surface, and your mind has been cleared of all illusion. You can now see things clearly and understand that good things, in the shape of beauty, are around you every second of the day, wherever you are.

June Angels

This is the traditional month in which to get married and go on holiday. It's no surprise, then, that the angel of the month is Muriel. Muriel is a symbol of balance and harmony, and this is what a good marriage depends on. Summer has come and with it the blossoming of Nature. If your partnership is blessed by Muriel, then as a couple you'll be able to walk forward hand in hand, trustingly. If you're planning a honeymoon or just a holiday, Muriel will help you enjoy your break in a way that will enhance your experiences and not leave you thirsting for more fun or culture or rest. Your trip, like your marriage, will leave you feeling satisfied and at peace if you use this angel's gifts.

ANGEL CHUTZPAH

If you are going to be a June bride or groom, then why not arrange your wedding ceremony with a little angel chutzpah and make your day a great one? Use an angel theme to decorate your reception hall. You can get the caterers to mix a new 'angel wing cocktail' with a tiny halo on a stick instead of an umbrella. There are lots of ways to bring angels into the ceremony, and it doesn't matter if they seem trivial. It's actually impossible to trivialize angels, and all these reminders of them will keep your energy on track. These little touches might make some people smile, but smiling is good! Don't forget, this day is about your marriage and nothing and nobody else.

Peggy told me about her angel-inspired wedding and she won't mind if you copy some of her ideas, even if most of them were forced upon her!

> Ever since I was a little girl I dreamed of having a wedding in June with all the trimmings. For years before I met Ari, I could see my wedding dress in all its glory. I already knew what colour bridesmaids' dresses I was going to choose as well. I pictured my groom in top hat and tails and it was all perfect. It did end up perfect, but not how I'd assumed. Instead of pomp and ceremony it was full of love and emotion and was a day I'll never, ever forget.
>
> I got a dress that was just as I'd imagined. It had a full, white skirt with many layers of petticoats underneath. The skirt had a spray of tiny silver leaves that swept across the front and from left to right. The bodice was fitted with a sweetheart neckline. I wore a single ruby on a silver chain around my neck (a gift from Ari) and a tiara that

sparkled with tiny clear and red crystals. The bridesmaids' dresses were a rich red, too. Ari refused the morning suit but he looked wonderful all the same. That was all as I'd dreamed – the rest was where it all went 'wrong'.

The day before the ceremony on 12 June, the church got flooded, as did the reception hall. We got the phone call at 4 p.m. I was devastated, as you can imagine. We tried finding another venue, but of course there was nothing available, or nothing we could find. It was hopeless. Phoning the caterers and telling them to cancel the meal was one of the saddest moments of my life. We'd also booked a band, of course, and we had to cancel them, too. I cried myself to sleep, and as I fell asleep I was thinking of the angels, who have always been with me, and I begged for their help. As I slept, I saw the most amazing thing: I saw my wedding as if I were floating above it on angel's wings, and I could feel the angels' love for me all around me. I knew exactly what I had to do. The angels had shown me what was going to happen and I believed them!

I got out of bed (it was still only 8 p.m. by then), got out the phone book and literally started sticking pins in it. The first pin went into the number for our local pub. I'd never tried them – the pub was too small and didn't serve food, but I called them to discover that they had a marquee up in the garden that had been booked for a family event that had been cancelled. I reserved it and started pin-sticking again. I stuck the pin into the number of a DJ who, when I phoned, turned out to be someone I'd known from senior school, who specialized in playing all the stuff from those years we'd spent there. I did have one hitch when I tried to re-book the caterers, as they'd already arranged something else. June is a popular month for weddings, after all. Then I stuck the pin into some take-away restaurants – maybe I was guided there… who knew what I was thinking! An Indian restaurant said they'd be happy to help, so a rather unusual meal with curry and poppadoms was arranged for my 50 guests. My mum and future mum-in-law promised to have the marquee suitably decorated in time, and the 'dads' were going to trawl the local supermarkets and off-licences for booze to replace what the caterers had been going to bring, so things were looking up. All that was left was somewhere to actually get married! Back to the phone book. I discovered that it was possible for us to get married, with the vicar in attendance, at a lovely hotel. Of course they couldn't do the whole wedding and reception, but they could let us use their ceremony room if we could get everyone there before a wedding that was already scheduled.

Ari and I spent the rest of the evening phoning guests and telling them of the change of time and places. The

ceremony went off without a hitch, even if we did all
have to travel in friends' cars. They made such an effort
decorating them that a Rolls Royce wouldn't have felt any
better! When I saw the inside of the marquee, I couldn't
believe it. You see, one of my dreams was to go to an
Indian wedding. I just loved all the bright decorations,
the special, joyful dancing and the wonderful, wonderful clothes they wore. It turned out that the people from
the curry house had made my dream come true. Their
son had recently married and they'd brought all the decorations to the marquee for me. Even the 'waiters' and
'waitresses' (goodness knows where they'd roped them
in from!) were wearing gorgeous wedding suits. It was
totally amazing. So, that was how I arranged my dream
wedding in less than 24 hours, with a little help from my
friends and angels, both spiritual and human!

Peggy's angel gave me the name *Eban*, which means 'rock-
like' in Hebrew. It seems to me there was no way this wedding wasn't going to happen.

Here is another holiday-related tale from Michelle
Corrigan:

I was lying awake, unable to sleep in the middle of the
night. My son Sam, who was then eight, and my step-

daughter Rochelle, who was 16, were due to fly from London to Bangkok the following day to visit Sam's dad in Thailand. I had booked them as 'unaccompanied children' so they would have help going through passport control and boarding and getting off the plane, but I was still worried. Things went through my mind, such as what if the flight gets diverted? What if it experiences turbulence and they're scared or get thrown around or, worst of all, are involved in a crash? What if Sam's dad gets delayed picking them up from the airport and there's no one there to meet them? What if they cross the busy roads in Bangkok and they get hit by a car? What if one of them gets hit by the motorcyclists who often fly through markets and on pavements, on their mopeds, at top speed? What if they have trouble when swimming in the sea when they get to Phuket and get caught in the currents? What if they get ill from the food?

I was going insane with all these thoughts going through my mind, when I suddenly thought of the angels. So I called in archangel Michael and prayed for him to protect Sam and Rochelle on their trip to Thailand and to bring them home safely.

The next thing I knew, the whole room lit up with a brilliant white energy. I looked over in the direction of the window and saw a magnificent angel carrying a sword.

I blinked my eyes a few times and then the vision dis-
appeared. My heart centre suddenly felt warm and full
of tremendous comfort. I knew that archangel Michael
would be watching over Sam and Rochelle, and I spent
the next fortnight with a peaceful mind. Needless to say,
both the children returned from their trip very happy and
healthy.

This time I have been given the name of Michelle's angel,
Erardo, which is of Germanic origin and means 'passion-
ately strong'. I don't think Michelle knows just how much
inner power and strength she has. Let me put it this way:
if you need a friend who will never let you down, try
Michelle. You won't be disappointed.

STRATEGIES FOR JUNE
SUMMER FLING
No matter what troubles you have and how insurmount-
able they may seem, make yourself a promise that even if
you can't afford to go on holiday, you'll spend at least one
week this month not worrying. It's been proven that when
you concentrate on something very hard, you can actually
make it more likely to happen. By thinking about worries
and filling your energy with them, it can appear that you
are wishing them to come true. So, for at least a week,

lock all your troubles away in a mental filing cabinet and do anything you find to be fun. Not all fun costs money. It can be fun to sit in a seaside café with a cup of tea and imagine the lives of all the people passing by. It can be fun to window-shop with a friend and imagine what you'd buy if money (and sense) were no object. It can be fun to use your imagination and write a story about your perfect idea of how your life should be. When the week is over, you may be surprised at what has changed in your life for the better while you weren't looking.

HAPPY EVER AFTER

If you and your partner really love each other, then happy ever after is a given. You may go through difficulties and you may end up being prematurely parted by illness or accident, but you won't hurt each other to the point of deliberate separation. Take infidelity, for instance. If you really love your partner, no matter what the 'chemical' temptations, you just will not risk the hurt it would inflict to give in to them for a few hours' pleasure. Make it a ritual for closeness and bonding that you never go to sleep angry and, at least once a week, sit down together and listen as you tell each other all that you've felt, endured and enjoyed throughout the week. No holds barred and total honesty is required.

TRAVEL LIGHT

Many people are afraid of flying, and I can't blame them as
I was once one of them. The thing to do is release that fear
and hand responsibility over to your angel. We all want to
let go of fear, but it's sometimes difficult to do. Imagine
all your fears as excess baggage you're having to take with
you, not just onto the aircraft but for the whole holiday. If
you start off with all that weight, then you'll have to keep
on carrying it. Tell your angel that he or she must take the
baggage for you. Feel your spirits lighten as it's lifted from
you and you end up with a lightness of heart and knowledge that things will all be taken care of and you'll be safe.
Board the aircraft with total trust, if not in the plane and
the pilot, then in the co-pilot you've hired: your angel.
Relax in the understanding that, whatever happens, you'll
be safe in your angel's arms.

WATER, WATER EVERYWHERE

When the weather gets hot and the humidity is high, never
forget that you need lots of water. Roughly 75 per cent of
the human body is water and it's no coincidence that 75
per cent of the planet is covered with water, too. This is a
message. As well as drinking plenty of water, it's a good idea
to 'bless it'. The old practice of 'saying grace' actually made
a lot of sense, and even more so where water is concerned.

Professor Masaru Emoto carried out experiments that showed that the crystals in water are affected by the different emotions that are directed at them. Benevolent emotions appear to create harmonious crystals, as opposed to negative emotions which create jarring, crooked ones. My advice is always to ask the universe or your angel to bless whatever you're eating or drinking. Showing appreciation for your food and water will also prepare your body better to receive it, and thereby help prevent digestive problems.

July Angels

July is of course the month for school holidays, and to make it all go smoothly and happily you'll need the help of this month's angel, Verchiel. With this angel's help you can teach your children to appreciate everything that is naturally around them. Animals, insects, plants, trees – all these things should create a sense of wonder in a child. If possible, take time yourself to show your children love in the best way possible, by granting them your time. Verchiel can help you see the world once more anew, through the eyes of your children. Don't always be rushing around, but take time to stop and stand back and just observe. This month, just over halfway through the year, can also be a turning-point.

ANGELS AND CHILDREN

Does it seem to you, as it does to me, that to a child summer holidays pass slowly, with long sunny days that just drift by? When I was a child, I was very close to my angels, although I didn't know that's what they were at the time. I thought of them more as invisible playmates who went everywhere with me. Children are naturally close to angels. For one thing, they have open minds and are not blinded by the same limiting ideas as adults. Children have the ability to accept make-believe, such as Santa Claus, and also the real, such as fairies and angels. Children meditate naturally every time they go off into a make-believe world of play, and this is why their vibration is faster than that of most adults, which keeps them closer to the dimensions of the angels. It's only when, as happened with me, they're forced to comply with society and 'put aside childish things', that they lose that connection and trust in angels.

Do you feel that, now you're an adult, the pleasurable days fly by so fast and the older you get the faster the time passes? The summer doesn't seem so long or so sunny. Nowadays children are dragged away from the power of their imaginations even younger, because they have machines in the forms of game consoles and computers to do their imagining for them. So many mums and dads become fraught during the long summer holidays because their kids are constantly 'bored'. They go to greater and greater lengths to amuse the children and, in doing so, they take them further and further from where they're meant to be. If only they resisted the lure of electronic toys until their children were older, their offspring would retain the gift of imagination, and so their connection to their angels, for much longer.

Josephine's Story: the Bathroom Angel

My sister and I were alone in the house – and in the bathroom. I was 12 and my sister was ten. While we were washing our faces, we put the plug in the sink and turned the taps on all right, but then one of the taps couldn't be turned off. We were in such a panic we couldn't even pull the plug out. My sister said, 'I wish someone would help us,' because by then the sink was overflowing. All of a sudden, the whole bathroom lit up because a bright light, which was too bright to look at, filled the whole room, but we weren't afraid. We felt this amazing calm feeling. At that point we heard our mum come home and she came upstairs because she heard us crying. We explained what had happened and as soon as she went to the taps, the water stopped despite her not being able to turn them off. Ever since then my sister and I have had a strong belief in angels, because we are certain that the bright light was one.

I've been given the name *Enfys*, which means 'many coloured light' in Welsh, for the angel in this story. I know that Josephine was mystified as to why the tap wouldn't turn off and then did so without help, and she perhaps thinks this was just some strange thing that didn't really mean anything in the long run, but I feel there was another, hidden reason why their mother needed to come home at that point. I believe the running water, which turned out not to be a fault, was caused to stop them leaving the house. I don't know what might have happened if they'd not been delayed and gone outside before their mother came home, but I do know that this angelic 'rainbow' saved them from something.

I had a dream of my own come true one July. And it really is connected to this book. Let me start at the beginning. Many years ago, centuries in fact, I lived another of my many lives. In that life I crumbled under emotional pressure and ran away from pain by committing suicide. I died because I couldn't cope with the very real danger inflicted on a loved one. As these things go, suicide is never a sensible option because the lesson we were meant to learn during those times will still have to be learned. So, when in this present lifetime my soulmate Tony was diagnosed with cancer, the temptation to 'run away' was there again. This time I held my ground, and in July of 2008 we were awaiting the results of tests that would tell us if his surgery had worked and if he was cancer-free. For years and years I'd been a writer, but had never managed to get a deal with a big publisher. My books were selling with a smaller publisher, but I desperately wanted to widen my readership, and to help more people. One night I had a dream – well, I say 'dream'; it was like a meditation, really, half-waking and half-sleeping. I dreamed that I was on a small boat drifting along on pools of water through interconnecting caves. One strange thing was that I wasn't scared. In real life I'm terrified of being in caves! In this dream I saw a beautiful being standing on the shore on the furthest side of the next lake and I paddled toward him. I resisted a panicky feeling as I had to splash and try and force the boat through the water more quickly. I stayed calm and, as I reached the shore, the being reached down and drew me up out of the boat and into his arms. I felt wonderful peace, a sense of all-knowing and that knowledge bringing a sense of safety and a release of fear. The being glowed with soft green light, and when I described him later to Mary Hykel Hunt (another amaz-ing angel lady), she told me his name was Gabriel. Gabriel is known as the angel of writers and a healer of emotional pain. Mary told me that he'd come firstly to cure 'writer's block' and also to reassure me that Tony would be fine. This reassurance had come to me once before, that time courtesy of a herd of mysterious deer, but it was very nice to get it again. As for the writing, well I wasn't so much suffering from 'writer's block', as the words always seemed to come, but perhaps 'publisher's block' – that is, finding a big publisher willing to take a chance on and have faith in me.

The next day, on 24 July, we were waiting for 4 p.m. to come, which was the time Tony had to phone for his results. I had sent several book proposals to Hay House a few weeks previously but there was no reason to expect an answer at any particular time. At about 3:50 p.m. an email came in offering me my first book deal with Hay House. I was ecstatic, of course, but my joy was tinged with apprehension about Tony's results.

As it turned out, thankfully, Tony was, and still is, absolutely fine. And so it has been. Bizarrely, every book offer from Hay House has come on the day of test results, or the day before them. (Tony has to undergo regular tests for five years after the surgery.) This has continued – to the point of being quite silly: I sent the last book proposal in several months before Tony's test was due, and I did that on purpose to try and break the cycle and give myself, just for once, a celebration without a proviso. But for some reason a decision on this proposal kept slipping between the cracks and being put back. You've guessed it I'm sure, but the actual offer didn't materialize until Tony's test results were once again looming! I've given up trying to change this now, as it seems that, for whatever reason, it's just the way things are meant to be!

Carey's Story

In August 2009 I was 38 years old and happy. I had a good job, nicely furnished rental home, new car, fantastic family and friends, and had survived a brush with cervical cancer the year before, but my love-life was a mess. I had divorced at the age of 32, and since then it had been a stream of short-term relationships – always great guys but always something not quite right.

I belonged to the social networking site Facebook and had recently commenced playing an online game called 'Mafia Wars'. To be successful in the game you really need to have a network of 501 people and, well, I don't actually know 501 people! So through a series of 'add me' pages I gradually added random strangers into my 'mafia organization' and was really enjoying the game. One day one of my fellow mafia members sent out an 'add Carey' request to all *his* mafia, in an attempt to make mine grow. I got 35 new mafia members that day, but I never realized that one of them in particular would change my life forever.

On my Facebook page my profile picture at the time was me doing a handstand on a beach in Australia, where

I live. Someone called Ted sent me a friend request, which I accepted, and he promptly sent me an email commenting on the pretty girl down under who was 'downunder', which made me laugh. Ted and I began an informal email exchange which turned into a webcam friendship within a fortnight. It was obvious straight away that there were massive sparks – but there was also a major problem: Ted lived in the States (in Texas).

Our exchanges continued daily, with webcam conversations and, oh my, we could talk for hours... I had found my soulmate at very long last. Late in the year I mentioned that I was coming to the USA early in 2010 to visit a friend. Ted extended an invitation to come and stay with him for a week to see if the massive feelings that were developing between us would be as strong in real life. I accepted the invitation, justifying to myself that the worst-case scenario would be that I'd found a new friend, but hopeful that it would be so much more. The visit to the other friend unfortunately faded away, which was when Ted extended an invitation to stay the whole three weeks in Texas with him. Ever hopeful that this really could be the one, I accepted. On 5 March 2010, and incredibly apprehensive, off I flew. I travelled from the Australian Gold Coast to Sydney, Sydney to Los Angeles (with an overnight stay) and then into Dallas. As I walked down the terminal concourse, my heart was absolutely pounding with nervousness. I glanced to the left and realized I was looking at a glass wall with my baggage carousel on the other side – and there was Ted. He was perched on a chair with his hands against the glass and had a long-stemmed red rose between his teeth. His smile made my heart skip a beat and I flung myself through the door and into his waiting arms for the most magical hug ever. It truly was love at first sight. ☺ Hand in hand, we walked out to his car, beaming like Cheshire cats, and the next three weeks were just out of this world.

The first week together was just Ted and I, and we had so much fun hanging out together that we even fitted in an overnight trip to Kansas to attend a Bon Jovi concert. On the Friday at the end of the first week, Ted's daughter M came home. He has joint custody, with a week-on/week-off arrangement, but due to it being the school holidays, M was coming to stay for two weeks this time. She and I hit it off straight away – there was no jealousy from her that a stranger was encroaching on her and her daddy's time, just friendship from the 'get go'. The second week M and I hung out together while Ted worked, and then the third week was just me during the day while M was at school and Ted was at work.

Unfortunately, all too soon my three weeks were up and I had to return to Australia. The tears and emotions when they dropped me off at the airport were heartbreaking. I cried the whole 26-hour trip home. When I walked in the door of my home and rang Mum to say I was safely back, I could not stop crying. I was totally inconsolable at what I had left behind, and my home was now just a house full of stuff.

It had been decided between Ted and I before I left the USA that we wanted to spend the rest of our lives together. Due to the custody arrangements and the age of M, I would need to move to the USA to live, and leave Australia behind. And the first step in that process was to apply for a fiancée visa.

So we gathered all our bits together and sent off our application to the Service Center in Vermont. NOA1 (Notice of Action #1) confirming receipt of the petition was received on 14 April 2010. And now we had to wait for it to be processed. The advertised average processing time for these visas is currently five months. During that time you cannot call and ask how your case is progressing; you just have to wait. However, you can log online to a Customs and Immigration website to see if there have been any changes in your status – which of course we both checked on a daily basis.

In the interim my flatmate had moved out so I decided it was time for the house to go. I broke the lease, had a massive garage sale, sold everything I owned bar my dearest personal effects (now reduced to four boxes) and moved in with my best friend, who kindly offered my dog and me a home until we were ready to go. It was a really strange feeling: I had mentally distanced myself from the old but could not move on with the new until the visa was approved. About two months in, we received a letter from the US Government requiring further information. We had put a short version of a document in the package when we should have put in a longer version. This was promptly fixed within 24 hours and couriered back to the Service Center, and they acknowledged receipt on 17 June 2010. And now we were back to waiting. In the interim this particular Service Center was getting really busy so they were farming out June and July visa applications to another source and these people were getting approved within eight to 24 days. Can you imagine how incredibly frustrating it is to see people getting approved in under a month when you've been waiting for two and a half? I was having terrible trouble dealing with it all.

One week I was really down in the dumps. I was tired, sick of waiting, constantly upset and terribly fed up over it. Everyone kept telling me my NOA2 (the

Notice of Action #2 telling us we'd been approved) was coming, but every day was such a struggle. About eight years ago through the Internet I had met Jenny Smedley. I had added her as a friend on Facebook so that we could continue to keep in touch. So there I was down in the dumps, wondering when this was ever going to end, and I saw a post from Jenny on my newsfeed which said, 'Remember, your soul angel loves you unconditionally. They have to, since you are a part of them.' I commented that I could sure use any help I could get and Jenny replied and advised me to just ask, sincerely and trustingly, and that I might be amazed at the response.

I couldn't get that comment out of my mind, and that night after I'd sorted out everything I had to do, I sat down, cleared my mind and asked my soul angel when I might get my NOA2. I didn't receive an answer that night, but for the first time in a week I went to bed calm and smiling. The next day I woke up feeling vibrant and refreshed. Off to work I went and during the course of the day I had to phone the Australian Taxation Office to find out some information regarding a piece of paper I had lost in the move. The operator asked if I had a pen and paper ready and said, 'Your NOA date is 14 July.' She was referring to a notice of assessment I had received the year before, but the wording made me sit up in my seat straight away. She used wording relating to my visa application and yet we were talking about a completely unrelated subject – could this be the sign for which I was waiting? I went home that night and told Ted, Mum and my best friend, and even made a $20 bet with Ted that 14 July was going to be our day.

So 14 July came and went with nothing received. I was disappointed and low but resolved to wake up the next day and battle on. At 5:55 the following morning I awoke to the mobile phone ringing. It was Ted! He was screaming down the phone with excitement that our approval had been received... it was, of course, 14 July in the United States. I rushed online to check and there it was, stating, 'On 13 July 2010 we mailed you a notice advising you that we have approved this petition.' Double shock – 13 July when the notice was mailed was 14 July in Australia, but we did not receive the email confirmation until 14 July American time – my soul angel was bang on the money.

We still have a couple of months of things that have to be done before we officially receive the visa but it's pretty much plain sailing from here. Sometime in October I will be returning to Texas to live with the love of my life and his daughter. We also plan on trying for a baby of our own straight away. I cannot believe that I have been so lucky to find what I found, but I thank the universe every day and am looking forward to a life of love, laughter and happiness with my gorgeous Ted.

I'm very happy to be able to say that Carey and Ted were married, in Texas, at the end of 2010. I was especially proud of the way things went with Carey, because I know she won't mind me saying that when she first mentioned needing help, there was definitely a note of scepticism in her posts. She had never before really tried to call on angels for help, or really believed that she could, and as I am a designated 'seed planter', I'm very happy when I'm guided to plant such a fruitful seed in someone the angels know is ready to receive it.

Carey's angel has given me the name *Yahaloma*, which means 'precious gem' in Hebrew. Having known Carey for several years (via groups and emails), I have no doubt that she and Ted have found their 'diamonds', which will last forever.

STRATEGIES FOR JULY
HIGH SPIRITS
For better energy for you and your family, look up. The use of kites and balloons, the study of the stars and the moon, appreciation of clouds and birds – all these things

lift your eyes, and when you lift your eyes you lift your spirits, too. Don't bemoan the windy days that seem to spoil the warmth of summer. Buy your children or yourself a kite and take it flying somewhere spacious. As the kite flies high on the wind, your energy will go with it. If someone's driving you mad with moaning, put all that hot air into some balloons and release them into the sky. As the wind lifts them up, your troubles will go with them. Get a telescope and examine the wonders of the night sky. Seeing the infinity of the universe will put your problems into perspective. Lie on your back and study the clouds. Let your inner child join your actual children in seeing dragons, angels and elephants in their shapes. Let your children make up stories as to where that misty 'ship' above is sailing to. Using your imagination is very similar to meditating and the journey will make you all feel closer and happier.

SUMMER DREAMS

Summertime is perfect for renewing your connection to your angels. On a sunny day you can find a quiet spot and lie back, feeling the warmth melt your bones away with your worries. This blissful energy is wonderful for bringing you closer to your angels. The countryside always looks more beautiful in summer, too, with sun-washed valleys and water that sparkles with a million diamonds. When you gaze at beautiful scenery, encourage a feeling of love for the country, the world and the universe, for these feelings will also bring you closer to the angels and therefore closer to your dreams coming true.

HOME IS WHERE THE HARMONY IS

How can you fill your home with the right kind of energy to invite angelic harmony for you and all your family, especially through the long summer holidays? The simplest way to do this is with uplifting music. Not the kind that rattles the eardrums! Music that always uplifts you is the same kind that always gets your feet tapping and has you 'dancing' round the house. If the youngsters in the house like heavy stuff, then set limits on when and for how long they can play it. Dark music will create dark energy if it's used too much.

HONESTY HOUR

With our busy lives it's too easy to let days and weeks go by without any real communication among the family. Surprisingly, forging a tighter connection between you and your loved ones also attracts a closer connection between all of you and all of your angels. So, for at least one hour a month, try the following ritual.

The whole family must lie on the floor, in a circle, with their heads in the centre. Everyone must take a turn to say something that has upset them during the week and name someone in the family who has upset them. They must also say something good that has happened to them. The rules are simple: everyone must be totally honest and non-judgemental, and everything said in the honesty hour *stays* in the honesty hour.

August Angels

You might feel tired during the heat of high summer, but angels can bring you lovely crystal elixirs to refresh your body and spirit. The angel Hamaliel is this month's guardian and as such can give you revitalized energy to continue on your path for the year with vigour and determination. If your mind has become clogged with detail and you really are 'sweating the small stuff', Hamaliel can come to your rescue. With this angel's help you'll get the clarity of mind you need to complete tasks for which you feel heavy responsibility. Hamaliel has endless patience so if perhaps you're struggling to learn to drive or need to pass an exam at this time, this angel is the one to call on in this month.

HIGH SUMMER AND HIGH SPIRITS

High summer has arrived! This is a time of many aspects. It can be a time of achievement or a time of rest and regeneration, depending on which part of your life you're in. If the year behind you has been tricky and the year ahead looks a little difficult, this is the time to sit back and take stock of everything you have succeeded in so far. Let go of anything that might hold you back in the coming months, and pat yourself on the back for good things achieved, no matter how small. This is also the time to appreciate your friends and anyone close to you. I always think August is a very good time for the 'pass it forward' state of mind. Even if for just this month, if you do someone a good deed for which you might ordinarily expect payment or payment in kind, then instead of accepting it, tell them to 'pass it forward'. This means that they will go ahead and do a favour for someone else without being paid for it in any way. They too should tell the receiver to 'pass it forward'.

August is a particularly important time for teachers as they prepare themselves for the start of the new school year and try to refresh their ideas so that they'll be able to engage their pupils with enthusiasm for their particular subject. Teachers have huge responsibility in bringing up the next generation, and their support can literally change lives.

John's Story

I was teaching in a very rough area in a US city, and the students were tricky to say the least. I'd found that it didn't do to corner these kids. If you tightened the chain too tight, then like nervy pitbulls they'd bite back. I developed a strategy for the worst cases. I told the class that I understood they were under a lot of pressure and so I was going to cut them a little slack. I said that if they found they were starting to see red and about to lose control, they could get up and go stand outside the door for a while. It might sound lax if you're someone who's teaching 'normal' kids, but it worked for me. Sure, occasionally one of them would take advantage and disappear entirely for the day, but mostly they'd just stand outside for ten minutes and come back in. It was a safety valve and stopped a lot of them 'blowing', I'm sure. Anyway, there was this one kid – pretty quiet for a change – who didn't mouth off as much as the others. He had a terrible home, I knew, and was often carrying bruises, and he had obvious cigarette burn scars, too. One day in particular he seemed really down. As he left the class that day I had a bad feeling about him. Something told me that he and I should stay 'in touch', so I stopped him and asked him for his cellphone number. He was puzzled, but I fed him some line about maybe needing to talk to him about his last assignment and he took that.

After he walked out, I wondered what had made me do that, but I had no clue. That night I went to bed early, as I was exhausted, and I had a dream. I dreamed that there was an angel sitting on my bed. I kid you not: a real winged angel, all glowing. He spoke to me and told me that 'Chad' (that's what I'll call the student) needed me to phone him. The angel said I would change Chad's life if I called him and then I woke up. It was 3 a.m. and I hesitated – I mean, what reason could I give the kid for calling him in the middle of the night? But still, I figured if he was asleep his cell would be off, so it wouldn't matter, and if he was awake, he'd just think I was nuts. I couldn't get the angel's voice out of my head – it was so real. So I dialled the number. It rang ten times and I was about to give up before it went to voicemail, but then he answered, with one word, 'What?'

I was lost for words. 'Er… hi, Chad, um… it's Mr… I just wondered if you were OK; I was thinking about you.' I thought, *Oh, great going, now he probably thinks you're a pervert!*

But Chad answered, 'I'm… OK, thanks.'

We chatted for a few minutes and I don't even know what we said, and then he rang off. I went back to sleep. Next day, after class, Chad asked to speak to me. I was a bit worried. I thought, *What if he thinks I've got a crush on him? What if he's got one on me?* Nothing prepared me for what he did say.

He told me that when I called he'd been sitting on a tower roof, about 80 feet up, getting ready to jump. He said that he wasn't going to answer his cell but the screen was so bright, flashing with such a white light, that he felt he had to. Chad said that if I hadn't called he would have jumped, but after we spoke he thought about what I'd said – that there were good people out there, and not everyone was a scumbag. He said that in the morning he'd packed a bag, left home and found a room in a mission.

I'm eternally grateful to that angel because two years later Chad had become a happy, independent young man who, if his parents had any sense (which they do not) they'd be very proud of. I know I was.

I have been given the name *Visita* for John's angel, which is Sanskrit for 'bringing light to twilight'. This seems very fitting for someone who brought hope to a boy who was sinking into the darkness.

STRATEGIES FOR AUGUST
CRYSTAL ELIXIRS

These concoctions can be very helpful for health and also for spiritual balance. When you choose a crystal, though, do make sure it's not made of a mineral that will actually dissolve in water and possibly become harmful. I've given you some safe options below. The quartz family of crystals are safe and varied enough to give you all you need.

To make any elixir all you need to do is to take your chosen crystal or gemstone and place it inside a glass of mineral water. Stand the container in the light of the sun and the moon for 24 hours and the water will have absorbed the energy of the crystal. You can just drink the water whenever you feel the need, or you can use it in cooking to benefit the whole family.

Do *not* use any of the following as they may be poisonous or contain harmful substances: actinolite, azurite, bronchantite, chalcopyrite, cinnabar, conichalcite, chrysocolla, cuprite, dioptase, galena, halite, hematite, kyanite, malachite, marcasite (white iron pyrite), psilomelane (black hematite), pyrite, realgar (ruby sulphur), serpentine (new jade), smithsonite, stibnite, tiger's eye, torbernite, tremolite, vanadinite, wulfenite, zircon.

You *can* use amethyst, clear quartz, rose quartz, smoky quartz, milky quartz, citrine, agate, chalcedony, carnelian or any other quartz. These are my top tips.

CLEAR QUARTZ

This is the master stone, suitable for almost any purpose, and so is the most useful. Quartz can both elicit and absorb energy, so it's equally good as a restorative elixir or to calm overactivity. If your children are wearing you out during the summer, you can both take it to rebalance the situation. Quartz is also the best stone for communication, and all angels vibrate to it; if you're feeling a need to get closer to your angels, a daily dose of this elixir will enhance this. It will also strengthen your communication with those who have passed over. Quartz is easy to cleanse and it helps cleanse you in mind, body and spirit. The elixir should be steeped in the west corner of your home.

AMETHYST

This is the most spiritual of all stones and if you want to interpret dreams correctly, like John, this is the one to use in your elixir. As it can also help with decision-making, it's a good one for this pivotal month of the year, too. Amethyst is known as the gateway to the spirit world and many people have visions when using the elixir. It's also a de-stresser, which is again useful at this time of year. Very good if you feel things are going wrong, but also very good for stabilizing things if they're already in balance. This elixir will also be good if you're having trouble sleeping, as amethyst in all its forms can settle a disturbed mind. Used to bring change, this stone is best brewed to an elixir by placing the water in the south-east corner of your house.

CARNELIAN

This is the stone to help you move forward with confidence into the rest of the year. If you've taken stock of the year so far and need some help maintaining courage, this elixir is the one for you. If you are manifesting any physical symptoms that you feel are a result of disturbance in your energy, either caused by other people or yourself, the carnelian elixir will settle you down both mentally and bodily. It's also a purifier so any issues relating to body waste, or menstrual problems, can be helped with this elixir. Carnelian is also good for soothing tired muscles, so take it after doing any physical labour. Used to create harmony, this elixir should be left to steep on the south side of your home.

September Angels

Uriel is your angelic guide for this month. This is the angel who will help bring your plans to fruition, just as Nature is doing for the planet. As the apples and pears form on the trees from the buds that opened in the spring, so your plans and hopes will start to form with Uriel's help. This angel can mop up any little spills and errors that have crept into your life, and clearing them will open the way to a perfect harvest time for mind, body and spirit. If your ambitions lie in the direction of bettering your psychic ability, then Uriel is also the perfect helper for this, too. Uriel can set you on your rightful path in life, bringing you signs and signals to guide you on your way, even showing you how to make a complete U-turn at this seemingly late time of year.

UNCONDITIONAL LOVE

Some of my readers might remember the story of James and Pamela which featured in *Everyday Angels*. James was understandably devastated when his beloved wife of 32 years, Pamela, died, and didn't think there was any future for him on his own. However, his angels knew better, and this November (2010) I had another email from him.

> I have some good news to pass on (compelled to pass on). I remarried a couple of months ago – a wonderful woman called Anne Marie. We have so much in common, not least of which is that we both do Reiki, which is how I met her. Anne Marie briefly got to know Pamela and they seemed to get on like a house on fire. We both have a very positive outlook for the future and are presently doing up my house to move hopefully next spring. I also became an instant dad to three daughters and a son, and a granddad to my step-son's daughter. As Pamela and I had no kids, it's quite strange, but they are all wonderful and I love them to bits.
>
> As the saying goes, time and tide wait for no man, so I'm determined to get on with the rest of my life, and at the same time treasure the 32 years I had with Pamela.
>
> Kindest regards, James

Naturally, being a kind and genuine man, James was surprised at finding love again after loving Pamela so deeply. Luckily, I was able to reassure him that the angels had sent me a sign that this was definitely all OK with Pamela, and very much meant to be. The sign took the form of a dear Dutch friend, Wim, who also lost his beloved wife, Linda, prematurely. Linda was nursed, through Reiki, by a woman called Marianne, the letters of which are of course the reverse of those in the name Anne Marie. My friend Wim and Marianne ended up married to each other, just like James and Anne Marie. This juxtaposition of names was a good sign that all was as it should be. James and Anne Marie were delighted to hear this story – a 'wink from God', as James called it.

I have been given the angel name *Talise*, a Native American name which means 'sparkling water', and I feel James should take this as confirmation that his new wife flowed toward him propelled by angelic love.

This is Wim's own story:

It was in 1964 that I sat in the child's seat of my mother's bike as she drove past the house where Linda, as a young girl, was playing beside her mother in the front garden. For some reason I felt very attracted to what I saw and secretly I planned to escape some day and honour them with a visit, forgetting about my young age. For a few moments I felt like an adult, with very adult feelings, but soon my age took over and I never carried out my plans.

The next time I saw Linda was 19 years later, in 1983, at the exact moment she divorced from her partner. She was six years older than me, but that didn't matter, and several months later we started a relationship. But we never married. We even didn't exchange rings, because we didn't see that it was necessary to broadcast to the world that we loved each other.

I'm looking forward to my upcoming trips to England because Linda and I soon found out that we had a past life there. Maybe 100 or 200 years ago Linda was an investigator (female) in a laboratory and I was her sister, or maybe a close friend. We were not in a relationship that time, but the friendship was very deep. We worked very closely together in the same laboratory that was our own, or Linda's at least. We did this research together for years. We examined the permeability of the skin. For this we used frogs, baskets full of frogs. So this wasn't exactly animal-friendly. When Linda was old she became somewhat eccentric and a little crazy. But I was helping her then and understood her like no other (see the similarity with this life? We knew this long before now). Amazingly, Linda had a phobia about frogs in this life. This was so bad that she would even have jumped from a window on the tenth floor if someone had been chasing her with a frog. And I have been helping frogs for three years this spring to prevent them from being hit by cars on the roads they need to cross.

Linda was an energetic woman, intelligent and extremely creative. She always said that she had chosen the wrong job by becoming a teacher in handicraft. She needed to create for herself instead of teaching others to do it. One of the things she said was that she needed someone to work out the creations she had in mind. Her exhausting job, as well as many nasty situations in her life, caused her to struggle with injustices of which she couldn't let go. Slowly, her energy decreased and chronic fatigue became her everlasting enemy.

In 1999 she was diagnosed with cervical cancer. The specialists in the hospital proposed radical surgery with uncertain results, so her decision was to go her own, alternative way. This meant that we were left practically on our own, with a very lonely path ahead of us, as we soon would find out.

We consulted a range of therapists who, each in their own speciality, treated Linda, and we were given an intense study in the modern-day state-of-the-art alternative healing methods, such as electro-acupuncture, Rife frequencies, Tibetan healing and many other more, or less, trustworthy practices. To this we added something of our own: visualization.

I took Linda to an imaginary place on a deserted beach with... an ancient stone circle. This, Linda told me, was her sacred place of meditation in the cosmos. She said that everyone has such a place, somewhere. There, surrounded by six standing stones, she would lay on a seventh: a strangely engraved stone in the middle, shone upon by a beam of healing light, originating from the Pleiades. What was remarkable was that when in the second year of her illness she suffered severe pains, this place accomplished what hardly any medicine could do: it relieved her pains, enabling her to sleep a little.

The scenery of these visualizations was initially made up in my imagination, and she filled in the details as she saw them with her inner eye. But what occurred after a number of sessions was that Linda felt a presence beside her. After a while this presence appeared to be a beautiful woman in a long dress. She gave her name as Amà, and she was Linda's friend. Linda had always longed to have an intimate friend, like a sister, with whom she could laugh and have fun. This woman really was one! Together they could run along the beach, feet splashing in the water. Sometimes, when Linda's head was filled with scary thoughts, she would ask Amà to blow them out of her head and, as Amà did, Linda instantly felt relieved. Amà knew many tricks to fight against the cancer and was very clever.

Together Linda and I fought against an army of nasty little cancer cells, but two of these creatures were very smart and withstood our efforts. When Amà appeared and we told her what we were doing, she told these last two monsters that a bit further away on the beach was an ice-cream vendor with the best sorbets ever. That talked them round and they took off immediately. Linda and Amà laughed at them, because once outside the stone circle there was no coming back.

On another occasion I was working to free Linda's belly of this big ball of sickening energies without much success, when Amà entered the visualization. I told her about it and Amà answered, 'What ball?' And she took it up and kicked it so hard that it rocketed straight out of the atmosphere.

'Wow,' Linda said, impressed by Amà's skills. 'She must be a hell of a football player!'

The first year of Linda's illness was rather easy, but one day she suddenly started suffering from very heavy bleeds, losing litres of blood, and from then on she started suffering from pains that were impossible to suppress, preventing her (and me) from sleeping. From then on our days were filled with fighting against pain and trying to get some sleep, but whatever we tried, nothing worked. Or it worked for one or two days, but then it was as if a higher force intervened and it was swept out of our hands. Disappointed and with growing desperation, our fight had changed into a hell of bleeding, pain, misery and loneliness, sometimes without sleeping for days in a row.

In a 'normal' situation the physicians would consider this intolerable and Linda would have been given numerous painkillers, anti-depressants, beta blockers, chemo preparations, etc., but communications with the official medical circuit were minimal, caused in some ways by our own attitude. Due to this Linda was so exposed to her sickness that it caused her to be confronted with deeply hidden pains of her soul...

At first we didn't recognize it as such, but over a couple of weeks she developed a habit of uttering strange words and phrases. I thought it might be some kind of distraction from her lonely fight against pain from which no one could protect her. These words sounded like they might have originated from Russia somehow and at first they were incomprehensible, but as the weeks passed by this gibberish changed into a very orderly language with words that came back at logical moments. She even sang complete songs in this language, with repeating refrains and melodies that were stunningly beautiful but never heard of before. Some songs were like marching melodies, others were lullabies, and yet others were real love songs that made me silently cry as I listened.

There was something strange to this language, because Linda's face changed while she spoke. It was as though her whole personality changed, like she was taken over by a... voice. At first we thought she was obsessed by some evil entity taking pleasure in her pain, but soon we discovered that it was something of her.

One of the words she often repeated was *nasja*. Every time she spoke this, it came out very emotionally. I was surprised to find out how much emotion, sorrow and pain could be put in just one single word, but with this word *nasja* a lot of tears seemed connected. Soon she combined this word with another word: *uzbekija*. And then she said *nasja uzbekija*.

We found out that *nasja* was a name, and that *uzbekija* means 'Uzbekistan'. We presumed that her voice's name was Nasja, and he or she came from Uzbekistan, but after some days or weeks Linda said that this wasn't exactly true. Often she could feel what was meant by the words she was speaking and suddenly she knew somehow that Nasja had been someone's wife. But who was Nasja to this person? Why was he so emotional about her? What had happened to Nasja?

One day a letter arrived from a woman who had been consulted about this by Linda's parents. This woman was said to be capable of making contact with the so-called

Akashic records which store every event – even every thought – in the cosmos from every being anywhere. This letter was a short one saying: 'Russia, a past life. You were a soldier and fought with swords and axes. On the battle-field you got hurt and fell. Your belly was cut, your intestines came out, but you alone stayed alive for five days with no help.'

Linda read it and then she called: 'That's him! It's him! Now I know what happened!'

Then I read it and it unleashed something in me, because to my own surprise I started weeping and I said, 'I was Nasja. In fact my nickname was Natasha.'

This letter triggered very old memories in the two of us, and that same night Linda told me in detail about her 'voice'. She said her name was Igor then and he was married to Nasja. Nasja was seven months pregnant and he was so proud of becoming a father that he was practising lullabies for the baby. Then conscripts came to their town and every young man had to go. For weeks they were marching and Igor learned many marching songs. When finally they reached the fields of battle, they were given swords and axes, but these were no match for the well-trained enemy, so Igor fell. He managed to crawl to a nearby tree but they saw him and cut open his belly. All his friends had died, but he stayed alive for five more days, his hands protecting his intestines, crying for Nasja, but no one heard him.

After that Igor became a third person in our home, like an ancient time-traveller dropped into modern civilization. Very often he took over Linda and commented on everything, singing songs and often asking for Nasja. He didn't speak our language, but Linda began to understand his messages. After he had seen me using the phone, one day he grabbed it, pressed it to my chest and said, 'Ring Nasja. Nasja Uzbekija!' Explaining that this was impossible wasn't acceptable to him, so I tried a different approach. I said, 'Nasja is here! I'm Nasja. I reincarnated!'

Expectantly, he lifted his face. 'Nasja?' he said. But then he touched my beard and sadly he dropped his eyes again, saying, '*Nasja ni... Nasja Uzbekij.*'

Igor was well aware of Linda's health and our fight, so one day he even taught me for half an hour using an Egyptian Ankh as a means to ease the pain, but one day Igor grabbed the first finger of Linda's left hand and said a strange word. Then he took another finger and mentioned another word. He watched me closely and was very serious about it. He went on and took all her fingers one by one, mentioning different words.

I didn't understand what he meant, so he did it again. But it didn't ring a bell, so I started doing the same, taking my fingers one by one and trying to repeat the words, but I didn't get the meaning of this.

Suddenly, Linda took over and said, 'He's counting. He's counting to five!'

'So what?' I replied. 'What's this? Are we going to learn his language now, or what?'

'Don't you get it?' Linda said. 'He survived for five days on the battlefield! He's counting the days! He means... something has to be done really fast now otherwise I won't make it. It's the fifth day! And on the fifth day he died...'

But no matter how hard we tried, we were losing this fight, and one day Linda asked me with a weak voice, 'What can I do to let you know I'm... there? Shall I switch on or off some lamps?'

I thought for a moment and then said, 'I'll just know that you're there, but... would you inspire me sometimes?'

I had been airbrushing paintings for years already, but didn't have much success, and at the precise moment I asked this question, I felt this would have consequences one day. A few weeks later Linda died, in my arms as we'd hoped.

At the funeral I spoke these words, 'My wish is to be together very often... to be one.'

It was about five months after she died that I started painting again, and right from the first painting I felt something had changed. Now, finally, I was satisfied with the results. These were paintings that told stories and revealed their secrets weeks or even months afterwards. I thought Linda would inspire me to paint, but as I soon would find out, she had surprising other plans as well.

One day I met a psychic who told me that Linda wanted me to find and wear an old ring of hers. That fascinated me, because while she lived we never had given each other a ring. So why now? But I thought, *if you can give me a ring, why shouldn't I return the favour?*

I made a sketch of a beautiful ring that satisfied me like the paintings did, and next I did her a proposal to bond with me through this ring in love and absolute freedom, but of course I didn't hear her answer – I'm no psychic. But her answer came three days later in a stunningly vivid nightly encounter with her. At first I dreamed of her and after I woke up and started writing down what I had experienced, it felt as if she still was inside me, answering my questions faster than I could ask them. Of course I also mentioned my proposal and then I felt a very warm hugging feeling going through my entire body and I wrote down the word 'YES'.

But who was to make this ring for real? A goldsmith, of course, but to my astonishment the only one that 'felt' right said to me, after I'd waited six weeks impatiently, that this ring drove him mad and he refused to continue with it. That reaction frustrated me so much that in the car on my way home I yelled to whoever was listening 'up there' that this ring would be made! And if he was not going to do it, then I would do it myself!

Oops... did I feel someone laughing somewhere?

It only took one phone call to find the man in my hometown who trained silversmiths. The next courses would start in two weeks and there was one empty place left. Can you understand that I felt elated?

One of the paintings I made was a round one and it felt as if it needed some kind of symbol. As I did with the ring, I used iron wires and constructed a strange-looking spiral-circle. I copied its shape on the painting in gold leaf and showed the result to the only therapist who had been allowed to treat Linda in her last months, Marianne, with whom I had become close friends, and who was very sensitive to energies.

She was very impressed by this painting and we started testing its effect by means of electro-acupuncture on a few patients. The results were surprising. Instead of using the normal homoeopathic remedies to neutralize certain imbalances, this painting could do the same.

After becoming a silversmith I forged this symbol in silver and soon we (because Marianne and I now were together as a couple) discovered that this jewel had amazing effects on patients when they started wearing it. We couldn't explain why this was the case, but the effects were so overwhelming that we started to produce it in bigger numbers, selling it by advertising in Dutch magazines. By now we had been given a name for this jewel: *Akaija*. When searching the Internet, we soon discovered that *Akaija* means 'we' in one of the languages of Melanesia.

Soon we received numerous enthusiastic reactions from people being relieved of all kinds of complaints, and sometimes the changes were small miracles. Soon we discovered that whatever this small jewel did exactly, it always was related to the strengthening and rebalancing of one's energy system.

One day I received a message from a young woman who said that she had studied the numerology of the word *Akaija*. She said that when replacing the characters by numbers, this comes out: A=**1**, K=**11**, A=**1**, I=9, J=10 (9+10 = 19 = 1+9 = 10 = 1+0 = **1**) and A=**1**. Six times a 1! And then we saw it... 'We' are One! That was Linda's answer to my speech at her funeral!

Wim's angel is a powerful one, as are his pieces of silver, one of which I wear regularly. But I do have an angel name for him, which is *Salena*, meaning 'under the power of the moon' in Greek. I think this means that Wim should perhaps try designing some new pieces under the light of a full moon. This may produce even more exciting results.

Sometimes at this time of year we have to accept that we've outgrown people, actions or places in the spiritual sense. This is a good time to prune away any behaviours or people that are destructive for you, just as you'd prune your roses for their own good and to stimulate better growth and flowering next year.

STRATEGIES FOR SEPTEMBER
DEAD WOOD

If you have people in your life who make you consistently angry no matter how much you try, then this is a good time to let them go. It may seem harsh but if someone is damaging your soul, you owe it to yourself to stay away from them, because absorbing their dark emotions will only pull *you* away from your angels. Likewise, there are those who drain your energy. They call you up on the phone and you get a sinking feeling, as they only ever call when they want to vent a problem, and you know that you'll leave the call feeling much worse and they'll feel much better. Of course it's good to help others when you can, and you must never lose compassion for these people, but have 'caller display' on your phone and when they call you either don't answer, if you're not feeling strong enough, or call them back after you've had time to prepare by closing down your chakras and thus will not be allowing them access to your energy. (You can do this simply by visualizing each of the seven chakra points as a flower and seeing each one close down tightly into an impenetrable bud.)

CRYSTAL CLEAR

Place crystals all around your home to refresh the energy of all who live there. Despite all the books on the subject, it isn't necessary always to use the 'right' sort. I'm a firm believer that crystals will choose you, given the chance, so go for whatever appeals to you. Let your intuition take over and place the stones wherever in the house feels right. Don't be 'set in stone' yourself, though – study the effects of the crystals and change them around if it feels right to you. If anyone in your house has recurrent bad dreams, then let them choose eight special stones of their own and place them in a pleasing pattern on the bedside table. All nightmares will stop because every crystal will have an angel with which it resonates and, once your house is full of angels, no bad energy will be able to enter.

TUNE IN AND TURN ON

If you know or have been told that you have some psychic ability, call upon Uriel to help you fulfil your potential. I've found the best way to do this is to choose first a set of cards to use. These can be Tarot or Angel cards, or Dolphin Divination cards (the ones with which I started). Ask Uriel to guide your hand and eyes to the right set for you. Don't worry about studying the instructions too much, if that doesn't feel right, but just allow your thoughts to come up with their own interpretation of the pictures, symbols and words. Start off by doing 'fun' readings for friends and family, and before long you and your guardian angel will be working together to help people out with their dilemmas.

October Angels

This month's angel is Barbiel. If you ever feel afraid then this angel will walk by your side. Sometimes considered a fallen angel, his task now is to support all those in need in order to regain his own place. In Barbiel you have a being who will do whatever it takes to score points, so take advantage and don't be scared to ask for some major help. Barbiel can perform amazing feats of healing, so if you're ill or need a cure for emotional dis-ease, this is the right month to seek assistance. Barbiel will also bring great compassion to your heart, so if you're having to spend a lot of time helping someone else – perhaps someone who is about to pass away – then this angel will bring you the depth of feeling necessary to go about your task with a light mind.

KEEPING IN TOUCH

I have some stories to share with you about people who've managed to connect with their loved ones as they've passed or afterwards. Although these events didn't necessarily happen in October, that month is a time when we seem to be able to get closer to the spirit world, and not by using pumpkins! If you look up Halloween, which of course is on 31 October, you'll probably find that the most common definition of it involves trick-or-treating, dressing up, bobbing for apples and, of course, carving pumpkins into scary heads. The original meaning of this holiday is quite different, however. Halloween is based on the Celtic festival of Samhain, which was the Celts' recognized special time for connecting to those who have passed over. Samhain actually starts at midnight on 31 October and is designated as a time when one of two great doorways into the spirit world opens, and the 'dark' season begins. The Celts held that there were two seasons in the year: the light and the dark. The light returned on 1 May, which is another holiday we've taken over from the Celts as a cause for celebration.

Surprising as it may seem, even bobbing for apples, where you try and bite into apples floating in a barrel or bowl of water, actually harks back to old Celtic rituals. Apple trees were sacred to them, and the fruit of the apple was considered a potent element in magical rites. Once captured, an apple could be used to create a special 'spell' to bring the Gods closer. At the end of this chapter I've included some apple 'spells' that will draw angels closer to you and therefore give you more chance of their bringing through a loved one to you.

Jacqui's Story

On the day my mum died (3 June 2009), I was sitting at her bedside at the hospice. She was in a kind of semi-slumber and breathing in a really laboured way. I wasn't watching her for a moment – I think I was checking a text message on my phone – but felt a presence in the room. I glanced up and jumped to see a tall, grey-haired, extremely beautiful woman standing at the foot of my mum's bed. She told me she was the hospice chaplain. She had a soft voice and a kind of transatlantic accent. I said she didn't look like a chaplain and she told me she was part-time. We chatted for a bit: she said she'd met my mum a couple of times and got on very well. She commented on how glamorous my mum always looked and how she'd always admired Mum's large, sparkly-framed sunglasses. She wrote down her phone number for me on a paper napkin and said to call her if I ever needed to. She wrote her name next to the number: Mary. Then she walked around to the other side of the bed, leaned down and kissed my mum softly on the cheek. 'Goodbye,' she said. 'It was lovely knowing you.' Then, saying nothing to me, she kind of sailed out of the room. As she crossed the threshold, my mum stopped her laboured breathing. Four tiny sips of air later and she was gone...

Weeks later, I remembered Mary. I wanted to phone her – maybe send her mum's sunglasses as a gift – but had lost the number. I called the hospice: they said they didn't have a chaplain called Mary.

Jacqui's angel has given me the name *Rocana*, a Sanskrit name which means 'woman of rare beauty'. Now that Jacqui has this name she should be able to talk to her angel every day, not just at times of grief.

Shayna's Story

I just want to tell you about one experience I had which still makes me well up when I think of it. It started when we had a shop in the UK. Two brothers used to come in the shop every day. At the time they'd just lost their mum and of course they used to talk about her all the time. One day one of the boys came in and sat with me chatting all afternoon. At one point a friend, a girl, came in and asked the boy if he wanted to go out that evening, but he replied that he didn't want to go as he was tired after working all week as a gym instructor. His friend persisted, though, and in the end he reluctantly said yes. He'd told me that although he'd go out, he didn't drink and would leave early, catching the bus home.

At 11:05 that night I was in bed asleep when I was awoken by the boy's spirit. He appeared and tried to grab my hand, but I couldn't hold on to him and his hand slipped away.

A few days later the boy's brother came to tell me that his brother had been killed, but he was so upset he couldn't get the words out. I told him I knew his brother had died at 11:05, which staggered him because that was the exact time that his brother had been hit by a car and killed outright.

A few days after that, the boy in spirit came back again and asked me if I could please tell his brother that he hadn't felt any pain and that he still loved him. It was wonderful to be able to pass on this message, but it still upsets me to know he went so young.

I wasn't able to channel a name for the brothers' angels, as I have no personal contact with them and it wouldn't be right to do so, but I was given an image of a shooting star. I think this is a message that the dying boy wanted to share with his brother: that at the point of death he felt no pain, and that his spirit just soared into the sky like a rocket.

Kevin's Story

While we lived in Alstonville, in northern New South Wales, my wife Liz and I became close friends with another couple, and we regularly went to dinner at a restaurant with them. They lived on a farm and had developed it into a home business. One day Ron was knocked over by a cow and hit his head on a fence. Sometime later he was diagnosed with multiple brain tumours and, being a homoeopath, he was not prepared to have radiation treatment.

Slowly, his health deteriorated, to the extent that he was placed in a hospital. We visited him, knowing that the end was near, to pay our respects. It was a terrible shame to see this friendly and fun-filled fellow go downhill so rapidly.

About six days after our last visit, while we were both in a deep sleep, I was suddenly awakened to see Ron standing alongside my bed, as true as life! He was beside me for only a few seconds, when Liz woke up and asked, 'What's wrong?'

I told her that I had just had a visit from Ron and said, 'I think our mate may have passed over.' I felt he'd been on a visit to us to pay his last respects. I looked at my bedside clock and the time was 4:20 a.m.

Some five hours later we received a call to inform us that Ron had, in fact, passed away. I asked his wife, who had called us, what time he had passed over and she told me it was 4:17 a.m.!

It was a very eerie feeling, which has never been duplicated, but it was wonderful to know that he was now at peace and felt enough for us to let us know so shortly after the event!

Kevin and his wife Liz have many angels around them. I've met them once (so far) and they have beautiful angel energy surrounding them. On this occasion it was Ron's angel that brought the message. I've been given the name *Gwennol*, which means 'fast moving' in Welsh, and this is what Ron wanted them to know: that he can now move around freely throughout the universe with just a thought. He says, 'No more trains, boats and planes for me!'

Michelle Corrigan has another story to share with us:

My mum was lying in her hospital bed, dying. She'd had a long, great life and after three months in hospital she was in a place of acceptance of death, which was very beautiful. She was clutching her rose quartz angel, which I had given her, and she asked me for some healing. I closed my eyes and placed my hands in her aura and saw her guardian angels surrounded by white energy. I was told by the angels that my mum's time was near, and this allowed me to say my goodbyes and talk to her about her passing over into the spirit world. She said she would send messages via the angels to me to pass on to the family, as she knew that I was a believer in the spirit world and the eternal soul.

I then had a vision of Jesus Christ, which my mum found so comforting. She was beyond her body and was so close to spirit, but at no time did she get upset. She just looked peaceful and full of the love that is just unique mother love. My heart chakra felt like it was almost bursting both with love but also from this overwhelming sadness that she would soon be gone from her physical body. The energy through my hands had never felt so powerful and I knew that this was healing energy being channelled, in a sense that it was helping my mum to pass over into spirit.

Later that day, her family was there to say goodbye to Mum. 'I've had a good life,' she said. 'Now you lot go home and get something to eat,' and we all left her.

That night she took her last breath and passed over into the spirit world. Her angels and ancestors were there to help her go into the light. My mum comes to me often in my dreams and I know that she is in a beautiful, peaceful place and, although she is no longer here physically, she is with us all spiritually.

Michelle's angel on this occasion has given me the name *Adrastea*, which means 'one who never abandons' in Greek. This reflects her mother's comfort in the figure of Jesus, as one who would never leave her side as she passed over.

Kathleen's Story

One day, shortly after my mother had died, I got one of those inner messages that said, 'There is a rainbow,' so I went to her favourite park on Sinclair Inlet, and there was the most beautiful rainbow I think I will ever see this side of heaven. It's a very special place for being close to my mother.

So a couple of months ago when I got another feeling that my mother was trying to bring something else to my attention, I took notice. Along with a strong urge to go back to my mother's favourite park, I also felt that she was going to send an angel on two feet, who would arrive on the spot to tell me what it was.

I went to the little park near where my parents' home had been when they were alive. As soon as I arrived, I was taken by the idea that my mother wanted me to find something special. I went combing the area, mostly looking down at the beach and wondering what treasure I might find. I began to feel an insistent plea that I should be looking out at the water. I looked up and scanned the scene and was frustrated, wondering how I was going to find something in that huge expanse of water. I sent out a plea of my own that I needed a messenger to come and give me directions on where to look. No sooner had I done that than a woman arrived at the park. I'd never met her before, but immediately she just looked straight at me and said, 'There's a whale out there!' as she pointed to the west of us. We watched for a few moments and soon we could see the telltale spray from the blowhole, and the splash and the tail of a grey whale. It turns out that this particular whale comes into the inlet every year about this time. My mother used to love spotting the whales and so enjoyed watching all of the sea-life activities near her home. She made many trips to that park, taking her grandchildren there. So that park is a very special place for my mother and me. The meaning of the word *angel* is 'messenger', and in a very pure sense I think my mother was able to send one to me that day.

Kathleen's angel has given me the name *Enakai*, which is Hawaiian for 'shining ocean'. I think Kathleen should take from this that her mother has returned to the sea that she loved so much, and that Kathleen will always feel close to her there. It's a wonderful thing and I feel that every time Kathleen sees the sun rise or set over the sea, it will now remind her of her mother's love for Nature and that we're never really parted from our loved ones.

Allison's Story

In 2008 I didn't handle my dad's death well; I didn't handle it at all. I just blocked most of it out and still do. The day he died he had to have a tracheotomy (an opening made in his windpipe) to help him breathe, but apparently his organs started to fail and he was bringing up blood, to the point where he was choking on it, and as he panicked the trachea tube came out. My sister Sam was his carer, and she was there – and so was her daughter, Mary, who was only 12 at the time. They said he came out of his room and blood was going everywhere. I can't stand the thought of it, and I wasn't with him at the time, so I can't even imagine what it was like for Sam and Mary.

I was at a Christmas party for my son's football team. I think I knew I was going to lose dad from the first text message I got from Sam, which said, 'Get to Dad. Something's happening. He was bleeding and has been taken to hospital.' I left straight away and was about 20 minutes away, but I can't explain what happened with the time, only that I arrived at the hospital about an hour and a half later, and my dad had already died.

I do know that I'm the most mentally and emotionally like my dad, and I couldn't handle seeing him dying, and basically he couldn't stand seeing me wasting away, either, because I lost so much weight after he died, and couldn't sleep and still don't very well.

Recently (2010), I had the most amazing and odd experience. This was at sometime between 4:30 and 5:30 in the morning. I was in bed, really tired but still awake. My bed is centred on the main wall in my room, and to one side of it there's an old built-in cupboard from which I have removed the doors and in which I store my CDs, on top of which there is a small unit with a stereo. Around the outside on the doorframe I'd pinned up a couple of hats, one of which used to belong to my dad. It's a cream fishing hat. On the other side of my bed is an old wardrobe, or actually I think it was originally a coat cupboard because it only had hooks around the inside and not a pole for hangers. It has a mirror down the centre of it on the outside, and that's where I saw my dad, right next to it – well, his face, as clear as day, looking down smiling, looking as he was before the cancer wasted him away. I wasn't scared at all and he was there for ages, long enough for me to think about grabbing my mobile phone and trying to get a picture. But when I tried to take one – focusing straight on his face – even though I could see him on the screen prior to taking the picture, not one would come out properly: just very dark and flashes of light instead! I can't remember if I said out loud or just thought, 'Please let me get a photo; just to show Sarah and Samantha!' (My two sisters.) Then I aimed the phone at the wardrobe mirror and tried getting a picture of the reflection of what I could see, which worked! I also tried to get a few videos but they only recorded for a few seconds. Days afterwards, the more I looked at the pictures, the more I could see. On some it looks like there's more than one person there and some are not my dad. The wardrobe belonged to my dad's aunty Pat, who died earlier this year. She was my gran's sister, and my gran outlived my dad by nine months. At least I now have these photos to prove that my dad's still out there somewhere, watching over me.

Allison's angel has given me the name *Dusana*, which is Czech for 'soul' or 'spirit'. This angel was especially chosen by Allison's dad to perform this miracle for her. I know that I haven't been able to show you Allison's photos and videos, but I have personally examined them, and I can honestly say that despite my having seen hundreds of stunning photos, I have never seen any more convincing than these. They gave me goose-bumps.

STRATEGIES FOR OCTOBER
APPLE AID

To use apples to help your angel connect you with loved ones, peel the skin, cutting it carefully into the initial of the loved one to whom you'd like to talk. Place the piece of peel into a bowl of water so that it floats there. Light a candle and place it beside the bowl. Take a small mirror and hold it, reflective side down, over the bowl and the candle. Turn out all the electric lights and, by the light of the candle, gaze into the mirror. Let your eyes go 'soft'. If the angels are able to help, your loved one's face will appear in the mirror and you'll be able to talk to them.

APPLE TURNOVER

Another apple-inspired angelic spell is to cut an apple in half and carve your first initial in one half and your loved one's in the other. Put the halves back together and secure with a ribbon. Place this apple in your angel sanctuary (or wherever you normally communicate with your angels) and leave it there for three days and three nights. You should receive a sign from your loved one in that time.

FALLING DOWN

It can be difficult to open your heart if it's full of pain, and hard to generate even a spark of joy or happiness if grief or sorrow is weighing you down. I always say that children are very close to their angels, and this applies to your inner child just as much. If you can, even for just a while, return your mind and spirit to a time of joyful, childish enjoyment, and your angels will come closer naturally.

At this time of year, leaves torrent down from trees in a golden shower, especially when the wind blows. So why not play a game with the leaves by trying to catch them as they fall, before they touch down? Even if you are feeling sad or troubled when you start out, before long you'll be giggling and laughing just like a child, especially if you can persuade some other adults to join in.

November Angels

At this time of the year especially, angels can help you find fulfilment in your career, your relationships and in your family, and help you with any really serious threats. Adnachiel is this month's designated angel. He will help you generate honesty with gentleness to deal with family and relationship issues, and he will give you the right words and actions to use. He will also help you bring out your qualities of trustworthiness and reliability to help you secure your dream job. Many people tend to 'power down' a bit at this time of year, anticipating the holiday season ahead, but if you press hard right now you can get a jump ahead of everyone else in the career stakes. Adnachiel can help foster exactly the right amount of strength with wisdom that will make you irresistible to prospective employers and prospective partners alike. And if any family members are being unreasonable, then call on this angel and yours will be the compelling voice of reason.

YOUR HISTORY
As the year draws to a close, why not try and get to the bottom of your character by having some past-life

regression? In my experience there's no better way to discover your inner truth than by re-experiencing some lives
lived before that have moulded you into the person/soul
you are today. This kind of thing can give great insight
into ongoing problems you might have. Often these problems are actually created by your soul angel (the angel who
travels through each life with you and helps you decide
on the right next life before you are reincarnated again).
Adnachiel can help you resolve all these issues, gently and
without further damage, so November is a particularly
good month for this.

Melanie was one such person.

> I found myself at a stage in my life where I was wonder-
> ing where it all went wrong. I was about to be divorced,
> even though I still loved by husband. We'd arrived at this
> point in some way I couldn't really follow, but I felt I was
> to blame. We'd only been married two years, and I really
> didn't understand how everything had 'just happened'
> until we were sitting across a table with lawyers beside
> us. I was in a job that was safe and secure, but which
> bored me to tears. I decided to try past-life regression as
> a last-ditch attempt to see if it could answer my questions
> and point me toward a better life.

It was fascinating. I discovered that in the past I'd been married to the same man before. The romance had died in our relationship and I'd become bored, cheating on him after six years. I'd felt guilty because he'd worked all hours to provide a lovely home, and then devastatingly a month after I left him he'd become terminally ill. I'd intended to go and nurse him, but he had his mother looking after him and I just couldn't face it. It was only as he lay on his deathbed that I saw him again and realized I'd been so evil.

When I came round from the hypnosis I couldn't believe the kind of person I'd been. But the therapist took me through it all, explaining that my guilt from that life was not only pointless (as I was no longer that person), but also it was destroying the current life for me and my husband. I realized that I had engineered our current position for fear that if we stayed together the same thing would happen as before. I also realized that I was staying in a job I loathed to punish myself, for in the past life I'd allowed my husband to do a terrible job just to keep our nice house.

Now that Melanie understands her past, she can change her entire future if she wants to.

Other people have had different amazing experiences with their angels in this month.

Holly's Story

In November of 2003 I had just started college. My friend, her boyfriend and I were going to listen to a band on a Tuesday night. Before we left the house we heard a bang on the back door. Almost instantly, it seemed, a tall man wearing all black and a ski mask was standing in front of my friend and me, and we were sitting on the sofa. The man was pointing an assault rifle at us and told us to put our heads face-down on the sofa. I instantly thought, *Well, this is it, I'm going to die.* With this thought I felt I had to do something to prepare myself for death. Having gone to Catholic school for most of my life, I felt that what I needed to do was begin saying the Lord's Prayer over and over again out loud, and I grabbed my friend's hand and did just that. This actually was a little peculiar, because at that time in my life I had turned my back on God and wasn't religious at all.

As the man in black and his accomplices (there were about five of them) ransacked the house and proceeded to beat my friend's boyfriend until he was good and bloody, one of them suddenly said, 'Hey, there are two women here.' They told me, 'Stand up because we need to check to see if you're hiding something in your pants.' At that moment my prayers became faster and harder. The room, which had been noticeably very dark, suddenly began to get brighter. I, however, was trying not to open my eyes, because I didn't want to look at these guys, but I could still see a little. I began to have a feeling that I can't really explain. The closest word to describe the feeling would be 'calm', but I had goose-bumps all over as well. Somehow I knew that I was safe.

Another one of the thugs came in, took me by the arm and brought me in another room before any of his accomplices could do anything to me. He threw me on the floor. At that moment I heard something telling me what to do. I screamed, 'No!' as directed by the voice. As the man pulled me back up, I was directed by the voice to grab on to something – anything. I grabbed on to something... it was a pair of white wings... I still don't know to this day whether they were real or not... but this room, too, began to get brighter at that point. Then the man who'd grabbed me looked at me and told me that he was not going to let the others hurt me. Another man came in then, though, and slapped me, but the first man told him to leave me alone. I've always wondered why he had decided to have mercy on me. Could he have seen something – maybe the same thing that I saw?

After the thugs left the house, I felt as though I was still being told what to do. I told my friend and her boyfriend that we had to get help. We went to a neighbour's house and called 911. About five minutes later the police arrived.

Since that night I began to feel like there really are angels that protect us. My faith in the spiritual world has been reaffirmed. My friends and I very well could have been killed or worse that night. I am sure that something, maybe a guardian angel, was protecting us and telling me what to do.

Holly's angel has given me the name *Hehewuti*, which is a Native American name meaning 'warrior mother-spirit'. It certainly seems as if Holly's angel was covering her with a maternal protection, warning and helping her through this trauma, which could have been so much worse if she'd been alone.

Charles' Story

Charles was a Sergeant in Company D, Second Battalion, 18th Infantry, 1st Infantry Division of the US Army. He survived several incidents which should have meant his certain death. I feel the reasons this happened was firstly because it would change him into the person he was meant to be, but also because he had important things to accomplish, and so it wasn't his time to go. This is the first time I've had the honour to record the story of a serving soldier, and it proves that angels can be warriors too, when necessary. This was certainly a 'serious threat', and I believe Adnachiel may have lent a hand.

The year was 1969. I had been drafted into the Army and had to report for active duty on 2 January, the day after New Year.

I completed my basic and advanced infantry training at Fort Dix, New Jersey, took my month's leave and shipped out with a friend to Oakland, California, for deployment to Vietnam.

We flew out to Vietnam on a commercial jet – TTA airlines (affectionately nicknamed Tree Top Airlines) – and landed in Bien Hoa after a lengthy flight. What happened next was prophetic of my year's tour of duty in Vietnam, as the base where we were to land was under fire from the Vietcong (VC) in the early morning hours. The pilot turned off the cabin lights so we could see the action below and circled the base until the all-clear had been given.

During my tour with an infantry platoon, we pulled six-man ambushes most of the time. I would come close to death four times, and each time it was as though something of a higher power kept us safe from harm.

The first occurrence was during monsoon season. Victor Charles, as the VC was nicknamed, liked to move around in the rain and had been very active in a village in the southern province. They would terrorize a village with their normal tax collections and conscriptions for the military, so we were sent to intercept Mr Charles in a night-time ambush. On our way there we had to cross a swollen stream using a hand-over-hand technique via a rope strung between the two shores. We had all been loaded down with extra gear in case we got into a fire-fight, and as RTO (radio operator) I had my radio, extra battery, two canteens, 30 clips of M-16 ammunition (ammo), six illumination flares, two claymores (anti-personnel mines), and two cans of M-60 machine gun ammo. Needless to say, I was overloaded crossing the swollen stream, went under and passed out.

The next thing I knew, I was lying on my back on the opposite side with this new replacement kneeling over me. Billy had jumped in to pull me out. He was my guardian angel that day because he'd just got into our unit and was there only a few weeks before we learned he was only 15 and had lied about his age. He was a big farm kid from out in the Midwest, but was there long enough to save me. At first I thought this must be a lucky coincidence, but this was to be revisited again and again as time went on. Once they discovered Billy's true age, they sent him packing for home. He was there at the right time just to save me.

The second occurrence was on the bridge to Cu Chi, just outside the village of Phu Dong. We guarded the bridge by night, filled sandbags and performed full sweep patrols during the day. The sandbags were to be the protective base for our platoon's tent, adjacent to the bridge, but with all the patrols and sandbag detail, we were not able to complete it all in one day. Our platoon sergeant thought it best not to use the cots provided but to sleep on the ground instead until the sandbags were all filled and stacked correctly around the tent. That night it proved to be a life-saving decision, as a mortar round that fell outside our tent penetrated the fabric like Swiss cheese. We would all have been wounded severely or killed if we'd been in our cots.

The next occurrence was when we were sealing off the village of Phu Dong. The battalion's decision to cordon off the village, heavily occupied with VC, meant using dug-in emplacements from several infantry units around the village's entire perimeter, hoping to force Mr Charles out into the open.

The position our squad was to occupy had already been taken, so we doubled up in another. That decision saved our lives that evening, as the VC emerged from a trap door over a tunnel complex adjacent to the other position we were to have occupied. It was well camouflaged with brush and when they broke out, they killed all but one man in that position – a position we were to have occupied.

The last close call occurred on a company-wide perimeter sweep through the jungle, in which all platoons in our company were to follow elephant-style until we all got in line, then turn and sweep through the area hoping to flush out Mr Charles. I was on the radio with the Lieutenant at the back of our platoon when the point man for the group behind us fell and squeezed off 20 rounds of M-16 aimed directly at us. Not a single round hit, yet he was only 20 yards away and there is no way he could have possibly missed.

When President Nixon announced the pull-out of the 1st Infantry Division in April 1970, I had made the list to go home as part of the honour guard escorting the 1st Division colours back to Fort Riley, Kansas. I looked back at my four close calls with death and by this time was convinced my guardian angel had worked hard enough, so I got on the plane and never looked back.

Each night I give thanks for my second chance at life and, like Private Ryan, hope that in the end I will have earned it.

Charles' guardian angel has given me the name *Bellatrix*, which is Latin for 'female warrior for good'. I think he certainly had some help from this impressive female being when he was taken into a war.

STRATEGIES FOR NOVEMBER
FLOWER POWER

Cyclamens are an amazing little flower for bringing us some beauty and power in the cold winter months. They come in many colours, but for this tip you'll need a white one, growing in a pot. This should be placed on a windowsill, and you should place a coin (it can just be a penny) on the soil around the plant. The plant should then be left where it will get the best of the moonlight each night, to play its part in an angelic prayer that will bring you your heart's desire. As time goes by, whatever you most want will come to you, drawn by the magic of the white flower, whose petals are shaped like little pairs of angel wings. I did this ritual myself several years ago when we needed some financial help, and it came, in spades! It's the one way I know that you can actually ask for money and get it.

THANKSGIVING

Of course the US holiday of Thanksgiving comes along in November, and I think we should all take a leaf out of their book. Take some time to sit quietly and just thank your angels, without asking for a single thing from them.

This will please them and also boost your own energy and therefore your connection with them. If you sit and think, you're bound to find many things for which to thank them, and this gratitude will pay dividends because it will make you remember all they've done for you, which will in turn make you happier.

NATURE'S MAGIC

It's a very good idea at this time of year to bring Nature indoors wherever possible. Anything with berries on will work wonders to lift your spirit, but don't take too much as lots of birds rely on berries for food at this time of year. There are a lot of evergreens that can brighten your day and your energy, if you can cut some without depleting shelter for wildlife. Another good way to give your energy and connection to the spiritual a boost is to feed the wild birds that live in and around your garden. Helping others weaker than you is always a good thing to do, and birds give you the added bonus of being very entertaining to watch.

RED IS THE COLOUR

We're very lucky that we live in an area called the Blackdown Hills, which are as beautiful as they sound. The main feature is the predominance of beech trees. I know everyone loves the symbol of our country, the oak, but for me if the oak is the king of the woods then the beech is the queen. At this time of year something of a small miracle happens. On the day of a good sunset, the sky turns blood red, and because the light is angled in a particular way across the sky, the trees do too. Driving home the other day I could have thought I'd suddenly been transported to an alien landscape. The trees, some still with leaves (beech trees keep their leaves, sometimes all winter – another reason I love them), were glowing with red fire from root to crown. It was incredible to behold. Always look for these miracles yourself, because they give your energy a real lift.

HOME IS WHERE THE HEART IS

Whereas spring is the traditional time to move house, November is the time to make preparations to try pastures new. If you start right now by asking your angels to help you, by the time spring comes you'll be first on the moving ladder, having already sold your house and ready to have the pick of the bunch of the homes coming onto the new year's market.

Spend this month tidying up the décor of your house, even packing some things away so that your mindset is already in the process of moving. See your new home very clearly and describe it to your angel in writing. In this way buying and selling can change from the next worst experience to divorce, into a transcendental and exciting process.

December Angels

Hanael is the angel for December and reputed to be the angel of relationships, friendships and love. What better angel to have for the Christmas period, when we show our love and try and improve our relationships with friends and family? If last year was a tough one for you, take comfort that this angel is also able to 'unstick' things for you. You can use this holiday season to ask Hanael to help you get your life back on track and moving forward. This is the time of miracles, after all, so if what you need seems impossible to achieve, don't give up!

ANGELS, LIKE PETS, ARE NOT JUST FOR CHRISTMAS

It's a funny thing how at Christmastime people always reach for angels: glass ones, china ones, sparkly ones, fairy-like ones – all of them make an appearance, in Nativity displays, dangling from Christmas trees and adorning shops and homes throughout the country. The funny part is that if only people knew just how helpful actual angels can be, they might talk to them on every single day of the year, about all of their problems, and they'd find they can actually get the help they need. From little things like finding a parking spot in a busy carpark to major life-changing events like finding a soulmate or getting that vital job – nothing is impossible. Everyone has a guardian angel and other angels that are on their side too, but most people don't know how to connect with theirs or ask for angelic help in their lives. The main thing is to create positive energy, as this brings your angels closer. Sometimes the holiday season can make this difficult, however.

CREATE JOY

Christmas is a very emotional time of year. It's unbearably exciting for children. It's a time of joyful gatherings and ecstatic reunions. It's a time of parties, feasting, drinking and celebrating. For some it's a time of worship and of thinking of others. It's a time of thoughtfulness and choosing gifts to give with love. For some people, sadly, it's a time of extra loneliness and isolation, and for some it's a time of stress and of trying to make enough money so that the Christmas aftermath won't mean being in debt for the rest of the year. For all these people, angels can make Christmas happier, easier, less stressful and less lonely, if they only ask their angels to help them get through.

If you're like me, whether you enjoy Christmas or not, you're probably finding that for the most part it's lost its innocent sense of joy. You're probably fed up with being bombarded two or three months in advance, when you're only just getting over the fact that summer has gone by too quickly again. In the modern world, sadly, it's all about money and this is what generates the masses of TV and magazine adverts that make you sick of the subject weeks before Christmas actually arrives. Years ago Christmas was about seeing your family and catching up. It was about playing silly games and feasting together. It was sometimes about forgetting old feuds or arguments and letting bygones be bygones. For the kids it was about baby Jesus in the stable and the thrill of unwrapping presents.

The answer to this problem is to put the joy back into Christmas yourself. To do this you need to talk to your family about what you all believe in and about what Christmas means to you all. Have your children choose an old toy to give away in exchange for each new gift they receive, and explain that not all children have someone to buy them new toys. I'd recommend that adults visit a homeless charity or an animal shelter and give what they can either in money, or if they don't have any to spare, then in that most precious gift of all: time. This sharing of positive emotions will create the sort of energy around which angels love to be, and with angelic help you will be able to create some old-fashioned Christmas spirit. If you're alone, then pamper yourself, love yourself, talk to your angels and ask them to send you signs that you're not really alone. During the holiday, if you see something lovely, stop to admire it. Don't feel silly 'oohing and ahh-ing' at all the Christmas lights, and take comfort from the joy you see in the faces of others and the knowledge that you're generating positive energy in your soul. And again, if possible and if you're fit enough, spend some time helping out at an animal rescue centre or an old people's home, or a soup kitchen, where perhaps there are others like you who'll be getting no visitors of their own.

If you're with family, insist on putting all the expensive electronic toys and gadgets away for at least one afternoon or evening. Play the old-fashioned games that are enjoyed on a more immediate level and can be shared with older aunties and grandparents who may be a bit technophobic. Make sure everyone joins in and Christmas will become fun again. At my mum's house at Christmas we all used to play parlour games – harmless fun that involved everyone – with no computer games allowed! Those primitive, hands-on games can't help but bring you closer together, literally.

When you're feeling happy and are generating positive energy, miracles are much more likely to happen. When you read the next story, you'll see that one never knows what might be round the corner or from which unexpected quarter help might come. Some of my contributors for this book have asked that their real names be withheld, and of course I have respected their privacy. 'Melissa' is one of them.

Melissa's Story

My parents had died when I was young – mum from a lung condition and dad in a motor accident. I was brought up by my grandma, whom I loved dearly. She gave me a wonderful childhood, but she was already in her sixties when she took me in, aged three years, and by the time I was 25 she was gone. I had her memory and, most of the time, that kept me warm, but as a supply teacher I moved about a lot. I rarely got a chance to make friends, hadn't married, and Christmas always got to me. I'd walk the streets looking in windows all lit up and cozy. I'd see families all getting together and it looked idyllic from the outside, even though if you believe the soap operas on TV, there were actually endless shouting matches going on!

I'd go back to where I was staying and the room would feel cold and empty of life. I'd always turn the TV on for company, but I'd tire of the endless babble and all the commercials aimed at families. None of it applied to me. People would sometimes invite me over – people from work – but it always felt like charity, so I always refused.

One day I found myself outside a church from which the strains of beautiful singing wafted out. It all sounded so joyful. I wanted to go inside, but something stopped me. Wouldn't they all look around to see who the interloper was? After all, wasn't the congregation just another family that wasn't my family, celebrating Christmas? I dithered in the porch.

This was a plain church, nothing fancy. I say this because I don't want you to think that what happened was a trick of the light reflecting in stained glass or something. There were no Christmas lights either – just a modest, carved wooden Nativity tableau inside the open porch. I looked down at the Nativity. The figures were a bit crude but there was something very calming about it. I don't know how long I stood there bathing in the beautiful sounds and the warm feeling I was getting from the tableau. Then I saw a tiny flickering white light. It was glowing in the tableau like a tiny little star. I turned my head from side to side and squinted, trying to see what it was, but despite its minuscule size it was too bright to make out any details. Then it seemed to flutter and almost, well, beckon me. It started to move, too, slowly across the Nativity as if visiting each wooden figure in turn. I leaned closer to it and each time I did, it moved nearer to the door, as if it were drawing me in. I couldn't help but follow it. I don't know why. I guess I was desperate for any invite and this looked like one. The little light slipped through the crack between the closed doors and I was alone again. I still couldn't understand it. I was thinking it had to be some little trick of the light, a reflection or something, but I thought, darn it, I'd go in and see what I could find inside this church. I opened a door, just enough to slide inside without being noticed too much.

I never saw anything more of the little star that had guided me in, but the church was so beautiful inside. It had been decorated with what must have been hundreds of candles of all different colours, as if perhaps the parishioners had all brought their own. Some people did turn to look at me, but they all smiled and I went forward into one of the pews. Looking to my left I saw I was standing next to a really beautiful man. I say beautiful, which would embarrass him, but he was – beautiful. He had shoulder-length black hair and he turned to look at me through thick black lashes. His eyes were honey-coloured and his smile wide and welcoming. I'll cut a long story short here (because the story gets a little too personal) and just say that I know now that it's never too late to find love, with a little help, and finding it at Christmas just makes it extra special!

Melissa's angel has given me the name *Ferréol*, which means 'can rely on/faithful' in Latin – a sure sign to her that she's not mistaken about the love to which she was led at Christmas, and that the relationship she found will be long, happy and true.

FINDING LOVE

It's quite amusing sometimes that some of us spend our whole lives desperately looking for love when in fact if we just paused and stood still, watching and listening for a while, love would find us! Tony and I got together between October and Christmas in 1967. We first met at a Halloween dance, when both of us were with some-one else. I can picture the white sweater he was wearing, and how it accentuated his dark good looks, brown eyes and tall, slim frame. He can remember my fun-coloured bright orange dress and my long hair. We were introduced to each other and both admitted later we'd felt a spark but, as I said, we were both there with other people.

Then we just kept bumping into each other. I did a 15-mile walk for charity a couple of weeks later, and who should be manning the drink stop for our particular group? Yes, it was the tall, dark stranger again. Then I went to a party, and who should end up sitting next to me? Tony again. It seemed that we were both attracted all along and maybe something about the depth of that attraction, far surpassing just a chemical reaction, made us both pull back from the inevitable. But eventually, Tony asked me to a Christmas party, and from that day to this we've been inseparable. When we met, I was just 17 and he was 19, and we were engaged six months later. We were married when I was 19 and he was 21. To us at the time we were adults – now, of course, when I look back I can see why our parents were worried, for to them we were mere babies. However, it eventually became apparent that there was a past-life connection, although at the time and for many years neither of us was interested in or even thought about it. I often say to people that staying happily married is easy – all you have to do is marry the right person. Of course the difficulty is *finding* the right person and realizing their importance when you do. It seems to me that people who are 'right' and will always stay faithful, and together, are first of all led, as we were (over and over again!), to find the connection, and they will have almost always been together before in past lives. The right partners have always made a contract before they are even born, with their soul angels and between themselves, to be together in the next life – and so it turned out with us.

It might even be a good idea for prospective partners to have past-life regression rather than seeking approval from peers and parents, especially if the partnership is controversial – perhaps where there's a big age gap, both are the same gender, or there are racial or religious differences – for who could argue with a couple who've recalled the same past life, separately?

Gill's Story

I'd been alone every Christmas, and this one was no exception. I had few friends and those that I did have had families, and were all excited about the holiday. I wasn't; I hated it, and nobody wanted to be around the Grinch! This Christmas in particular was especially grim for me because my cat had just died. I know people say it's silly to grieve for a cat, but she was going to be my only company that year. I thought about ending it all. I even went as far as collecting a whole load of pills, one way and another, and I sat there with them all lined up and a bottle of vodka ready to wash them down with. I contemplated why I felt so low at Christmas and I figured that for the rest of the time I could bury myself in work, always had work colleagues around me and I could fool myself that I had a life. Now I was sitting alone, everyone else off buying presents whereas I had no one to buy for – we'd done 'Secret Santa' at work and that was that. The office had shut down for two weeks and here I was contemplating two weeks of mind-numbing TV, TV dinners (I couldn't be bothered to cook for one) and endless bottles of vodka to numb the pain – what was it all for? What was the point in it all?

The phone rang and so I sipped the vodka instead of the pills while I decided whether to answer it. In the end what made me pick it up was the fact that I'd been moaning that no one cared, and now someone was calling. Not wanting to think myself a hypocrite, I answered it. (The fact that a loud voice, seemingly hovering in mid-air just by my ear, shouted at me to pick up may have had something to do with it – if you ask me about that later I'll deny it!)

It was an old woman I called Grandma Nutkins. She lived on the floor below me and I called her that because she was your archetypical grandmother, so cute and apparently with five children and 28 grandchildren and great-grandchildren. I had no idea why she'd be calling me – maybe she needed help buying them all gifts. Anyway, Dora, as was her real name, asked me if I'd come downstairs as she'd bought me a little gift. I was sort of pleased, I admit, but I hadn't bought her anything. I looked at my vodka stock – could you give an old woman a bottle of vodka for Christmas? I didn't know, but it was all I had apart from a frozen turkey dinner, so I swaddled it in some purple tissue paper I salvaged from the bin and off I went.

Dora was touchingly pleased with the vodka. I didn't know much about her – only that she was picked up by taxi every Sunday and came back Monday morning, having stayed with one of her kids. Anyway, she seemed keen to christen the bottle, so we shared it, toasting the Christmas season. It was nice not to be drinking alone.

It all went weird once Dora had downed a few glasses, though. She started to cry, silently at first, big teardrops rolling softly down her cheeks. I asked her what was wrong and that really started her crying. Pretty soon I could barely understand her words as she talked through her sobs. She told me something that blew me away. She told me she was alone, that she had no children or grandchildren, and that every Sunday she took herself off in a taxi and stayed the night in a hotel. She did it to pretend that she was loved, whereas in reality, she said, no one cared. She pointed to the photos on all her cupboards: photos of children and adults, all smiling at the camera. 'See,' she said, 'I'm not in any of them. They're not real. They're not mine.'

I was staggered, for here was someone even sadder than me. At least at work they knew I was a lonely spinster, but then I thought that it must have at least kept Dora occupied, thinking all this up and play-acting all the time. Right then and there I realized that someone had taken us both by the scruff of the neck that day – stopped me from a lame, attention-seeking suicide attempt and her from her life of lies. I resolved I was going to make a better life for both of us. I told Dora I was going to go and buy us some stuff. It wasn't too late and I'd get some bargains. That was when she rummaged around in a drawer and shoved £200 into my hand. I'd never realized that what Dora did have, and would have swapped for family in a heartbeat, was stacks of cash.

It didn't matter – I rushed off and bought a huge turkey and all the trimmings. I got a tree and some coloured lights, candles and tinsel, and by the time I ushered Dora up to my flat, it was like a proverbial Christmas grotto in there. We spent that Christmas eating, drinking and, believe it or not, making merry. It turned out that Dora had been part of a theatrical touring company. She'd met loads of famous people in her life and had some wickedly funny stories to tell, and she did.

I don't know what's going to happen now; Dora is 81 years old after all, but I'm going to do my best to obey that 'angel' or whatever it was and live my life as best I can, for me and for Dora.

Gill's angel – for yes, she has got one – has given me the name *Myra*, which comes from the Latin and means 'perhaps'. I think Gill's life is full of possibilities now, and it remains to be seen what she makes of them. I like to think that Myra will lead her and Dora on some great adventures and that, by the time Dora passes, Gill will have developed a life of her own that she can enjoy to the full.

STRATEGIES FOR DECEMBER
UNCONDITIONAL LOVE
Take some time from the hustle and bustle and experience love of yourself. Sit quietly and make your breathing regular and soft. Close your eyes and feel a warm glow coming over you, as unconditional love from your angel wraps around you like silken wings. If an angel loves you this much, then you should surely love yourself, too.

ANGEL LIGHT
Angels just love candles, and they seem to abound at Christmastime, so make use of the atmosphere they create. If you have any negativity in your heart at this time of year it can be especially painful, so make a deal that just

for at least these few holiday days you'll put it out of your life and your thoughts. Visualize your problems as dark little balls of fluff and toss each one into the flame of a candle. Let the light take care of those problems for now.

SNOW ANGELS

If you do get a sprinkling of the white stuff over Christmas, take the opportunity to lie in the snow and make snow angels by sweeping your arms and legs up and down through the snow. Write the name of someone you love in the snow. Throw snowballs. Wonder at the amazing unique shapes of the snow crystals by looking at them under a microscope. The winter world can be full of little miracles, and anything that releases your inner child will enhance the Christmas experience and may transport you back to a mindset when angels were your best friends.

BE AN ANGEL

Nothing delights angels more than 'random acts of kindness'. It would be nice if everyone practised them every day of the year, but Christmas seems an especially good place to start. If you're well off and you have money to spare, then try this: walk through a shopping mall and pick out someone who looks in need. I'm not necessarily talking about beggars here, but perhaps a harassed-looking mum who's gazing hopelessly into a toy store window and seems to be desperately wondering how she can afford to get her child something. Or an elderly man who looks very cold and is perhaps wandering round the shops just to avoid going home and having to turn the costly heating on. Take a note out of your purse or wallet. It can be any amount you can easily afford. Drop the note on the floor beside the person you've chosen, and then tap them on the shoulder, point to the note and say it just fell out of their pocket.

If you're not well off enough to do that, then just offer to help someone or just offer them a warm smile. That too can change someone's day and make you their angel.

A Special Angel for Every Day of the Week

Which angel is the one to call on for help on any given day of the week?

During my many communications with angels, they sometimes give me names for themselves that aren't always the same as the commonly accepted ones. I think this is because angels don't actually use names for each other; they use energy. The angels don't mind if we use names for them, as very few of us in our human bodies have the ability to recognize them, or other people, purely by the energy of which we are all made up. To this end, they have given me names to use that are different from the norm and, to me, anyway, very meaningful. I think it helps to develop a more intimate relationship with an angel if you have a special name for each one. It makes it more personal somehow. You might be able to get your own names, and do try, but if not, you can use mine. To help with this I've added these names to the ones below and I hope you agree that they're well-suited to the corresponding angel. These names seem to come from ancient Sanskrit. Some of the names appear to be female and I think this is again just down to energy. Female energy is of course very different from male, and the meanings seem to reflect this appropriately. However, the new names sometimes seem to change from male to female or vice versa, so I've used the pronoun 'he' throughout, just to save confusion.

SUNDAY

This is the first day of the week for most people, and this is your 'stock-taking' day. This is the day to ask Michael to come close to you. He has given me the name *Mohinder* (which means 'great'). This is the day when you assess your spiritual state to see if you're really developing as you had hoped. It's the day to be honest and open, and if you find you've slipped back this week, don't worry about being judged. Mohinder is a warrior and as such he can help you fight for progress. You can tell him anything and he'll always show you nothing but unconditional love. He'll offer you his strength to help you literally fight your own demons. All he asks in return is that you tell him the truth. He is a rescuer to whom you can turn when it seems you're stuck and not moving forward. Mohinder will help you stand up for what is right.

Michael/Mohinder has told me that the best crystal for this day of the week is a quartz crystal of any colour.

MONDAY

This is a day to begin creating for the rest of the week, and for this you call on Gabriel, who has given me the name *Asha* (meaning 'wish' or 'hope'). Just as he can unblock writers when they become stuck for words, he can unstick your life and get things moving. If you are someone who's been held back by social conditioning, or by well-meaning but disbelieving family members, Asha can create a shift. Asha can help you because he can bring clarity to you if you've lost or are seeking your true pathway and purpose. He'll bring inspiration to the depressed mind and open the way to new and undreamed-of talents. All he asks in return is that when you've unburdened yourself, you let go and trust that the universe will turn in its own time and bring you the answers you seek. Asha will heal the emotional pain of betrayal and help you purify your energy.

Gabriel/Asha has told me that the best crystal for this day of the week is moonstone.

TUESDAY

This is the day of Khamael, the angel of balance in love. I have been given the name *Karna* (which means 'will hear'). It's wonderful and important to feel unconditional love for someone else, but it's also wonderful – and too easily forgotten – to feel that love for yourself, too. On Tuesdays you can call on this angel to look back over your life at times when you've blamed yourself for events with which you weren't perhaps well equipped to deal at the time. Karna will encourage you to re-embrace your younger self and forgive them for what has gone before. He will help you wipe the slate clean and have a better life. This angel will remind you of the truth which is difficult to accept sometimes: that with all the responsibilities you have, you must never forget the most important one, the one you came here to really fulfil – the responsibility for the progress and cleansing of your own soul.

Khamael/Karna has told me that the best crystal for this day of the week is opal.

WEDNESDAY

The middle of the week, and as such the time to stop for a moment and take stock of the way the week is going. The angel of the day is Raphael, the healer of all healers. He has given me the name *Rohan* (meaning 'ascending', 'lifting up'). If anything at all has gone wrong so far, Rohan can put it right. This is a time to think back on any little signs and messages you may have missed or misinterpreted. Write anything at all that comes to you down on a piece of paper and meditate on it. You should see it all come together and solidify into something meaningful. Thus, things that have seemed 'wrong' may now seem 'right' after all.

Raphael/Rohan has told me that the best crystal for this day of the week is citrine.

THURSDAY

This can often be a turning point and a day when you're feeling particularly stressed and tired. The weekend isn't yet very close so you can't start to unwind, and yet there isn't much time left to accomplish what you set out to do. Cassiel will be a welcome helper on this day of the week. I have been given the name *Indira* (which means 'beauty'). Indira knows your true self and knows that you have the capability to become a balanced soul. This angel can help you if you're feeling tempted to take an easy way out that will harm you in the long run. Indira will show you your true potential and give you fresh determination to succeed while doing the right thing.

Cassiel/Indira has told me that the best crystal for this day of the week is obsidian.

FRIDAY

Friday is the day of Uriel, the angel most child-orientated of them all. Uriel has given me the name *Usha* (which means 'dawn' or 'bright beginning'), and he comes to remind you of the importance of nurturing and honouring your inner child. Children's energy is very special and Usha wants you to return to that being you were born to be. Usha wants you to shake off the social pressures that changed you and once more become open and accepting of the existence of both miracles and magic. This angel is one who exudes female energy to me, so you can think of Usha as a mother or as a sibling. This is the day to release a sense of adventure, just as you had as a child, and push all logic and barriers to one side. Look not on this day for the trappings of success; instead, look for joy only in simple things and purity of heart.

Uriel/Usha has told me that the best crystal for this day of the week is tiger's eye.

SATURDAY

This is the day for the angel of relationships, Haniel. I have been given the name *Karishma* (which means 'miracle'). If you've lost all hope of ever finding a soulmate, Karishma will show you hope. If you already have a relationship but are having problems, she will help you solve them. Family feuds can be settled on this day with the help of this angel, and if you do this, the calm energy you produce will only strengthen your angelic connections. On the other hand, if issues cannot be resolved, Karishma will encourage you not to take the blame if you've tried everything you can. Sometimes we need to recognize that a person, whether family member, friend or partner, is not the right person to have in our lives, and we cannot be afraid to take a decisive step away.

Haniel/Karishma has told me that the best crystal for this day of the week is rose quartz.

Afterword

There's a line from a song, 'You're nobody till somebody loves you', and a lot of people believe it is true. Well, angels do love you. They love every single one of you, and in reality they're around you every single second of every single day of your life. They love your soul, and this is something in which you need to believe. Angels don't need or use names among themselves. They don't call us names like 'Jenny Smedley' or anything else. They recognize each other, and us, by our energy, and that's all they need. To them our energy is as unique to each of us as our finger-prints and DNA are unique to us in the human world. They don't depend on it being a certain day or a certain time in order to appear; in fact, time has no rule over them at all. They don't have to appear in any certain way and can be seen as light, as a person, and even as an animal or a tree, or a rainbow or a cloud – anything at all. However, despite their not having the limitations that we have, they do understand that most of us need them. The fact is that we, as humans, find it easier to step into our spiritual selves if we have a logical pathway to lead us there. So if it helps to have a name especially for your angel, they're quite happy to answer to one. If you prefer a ritual to connect with them that feels right at a certain time or on a certain day, they're quite happy to go along with it. They do this because they love us – unconditionally and without exception. So do whatever feels right to you, and your angel will be quite happy to co-operate. There is just one immovable and irrevocable rule: always remember that to your angel you *are* somebody, you're somebody very important indeed. Never lose sight of that. Even if you have no one else in the world, or likewise if you're lucky enough to have other humans and animals that love you, your angel will always be beside you and will always want to help you. You just have to have the courage to ask, and to have that courage you need to feel their love for you. So if ever you have a moment of doubt, just stop what you're doing and close your eyes. Listen and feel with your soul, and you'll sense your angel wrap you in wings of love.

Resources

For details of Chrissie Astell's courses, workshops, books, oracle cards and meditation CDs, visit www.AngelLight. co.uk and www.Educatingheartandsoul.com

Diana Cooper: www.dianacooper.com

Michelle Corrigan: www.purplebuddha.co.uk

Michelle Jones: www.michellejones.me.uk

Frances Munro: www.francesmunro.com

Jacky Newcomb: www.jackynewcomb.com

Wim Roskam: www.akaija-art.com

Terry Ann Shuman-Gerspach: www.guidinglightproducts. com

Alexandra Wenman: www.vitalitypublishing.com

www.foresight-preconception.org.uk

www.sarielhealing.com

RECOMMENDED READING

Advice from Angels – Chrissie Astell (Godsfield)

A New Light on Angels – Diana Cooper (Findhorn)

Angel Secrets – Jacky Newcomb (Octopus)

Angels Please Hear Me – Jenny Smedley (Hay House)

Angel Whispers – Jenny Smedley (Hay House)

Everyday Angels – Jenny Smedley (Hay House)

Gifts from Your Angels – Chrissie Astell (Watkins/Duncan Baird Publishing)

Soul Angels – Jenny Smedley (Hay House)

Your Quest for a Spiritual Life – Michelle Corrigan (O Books)

JOIN THE HAY HOUSE FAMILY

As the leading self-help, mind, body and spirit publisher in the UK, we'd like to welcome you to our family so that you can enjoy all the benefits our website has to offer.

 EXTRACTS from a selection of your favourite author titles

 COMPETITIONS, PRIZES & SPECIAL OFFERS Win extracts, money off, downloads and so much more

 LISTEN to a range of radio interviews and our latest audio publications

 CELEBRATE YOUR BIRTHDAY An inspiring gift will be sent your way

 LATEST NEWS Keep up with the latest news from and about our authors

 ATTEND OUR AUTHOR EVENTS Be the first to hear about our author events

 iPHONE APPS Download your favourite app for your iPhone

 HAY HOUSE INFORMATION Ask us anything, all enquiries answered

join us online at **www.hayhouse.co.uk**

 292B Kensal Road, London W10 5BE
T: 020 8962 1230 E: info@hayhouse.co.uk

ABOUT THE AUTHOR

Based in the beautiful county of Somerset in the UK and happily married for more than 40 years, **Jenny Smedley** DPLT is a qualified past-life regressionist, author, TV and radio presenter and guest, international columnist and spiritual consultant specializing in the subjects of past lives and angels. She's also an animal intuitive and tree communicator. She lives with her husband Tony, a spiritual healer, and her reincarnated Springador dog, KC.

Her own current life was turned around by a vision from one of her past lives, in which she knew the man known today as Garth Brooks. Problems and issues related to that life were healed and resolved in a few seconds. For two years she hosted her own spiritual chat show on Taunton TV, interviewing people such as David Icke, Reg Presley, Uri Geller and Diana Cooper. Jenny has appeared on many TV shows in the UK, USA, Ireland and Australia, including *The Big Breakfast*, *Kelly*, *Open House*, *The Heaven and Earth Show*, *Kilroy* and *Jane Goldman Investigates*. She has also been a guest on hundreds of radio shows including The *Steve Wright Show* on BBC Radio 2 and *The Richard Bacon Show* on BBC Five Live in the UK, as well as in places as far-flung as Australia, New Zealand, Iceland, Tasmania, Spain, South Africa, the USA and the Caribbean. She writes regular columns for five magazines in three countries.

After being shown her Master Path by an angel, Jenny was given the ability to create Mirror Angel Portraits and remote aura pictures, and to help others connect to their angels.

She'd love to hear from you, so please get in touch by emailing her at author@globalnet.co.uk and perhaps your story will be featured in one of her future books.

www.jennysmedley.com